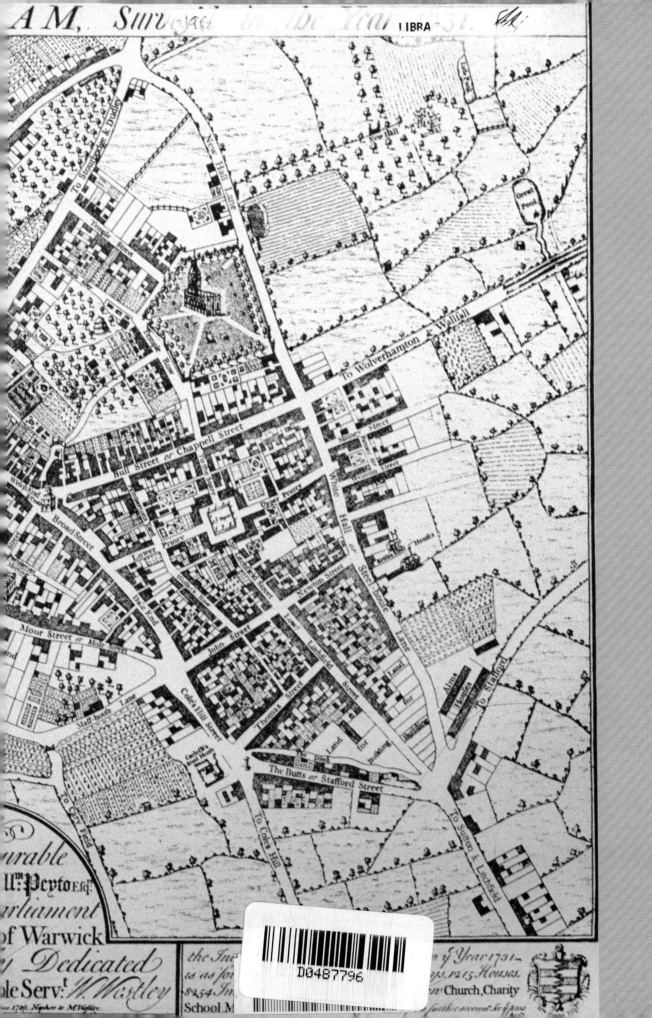

THE STORY OF

TY·PHOO

Sir John Sumner.

THE STORY OF

TY·PHOO

Ken Williams

QUILLER PRESS

Dedicated to the memory
of my parents

George and May Williams

First published 1990 by
Quiller Press Limited
46 Lillie Rd, SW6 1TN

ISBN 1 870948 289

Produced by Hugh Tempest-Radford
Designed by Gary John Robinson
Printed in Italy by New Interlitho (U.K.) Ltd.

CONTENTS

PREFACE

PERHAPS it was inevitable with my interest in local history research, drawing and painting, also having been involved in the Birmingham tea trade for over 35 years working for 'Typhoo' tea, that I should turn my hand to researching the history of 'Typhoo' and the Birmingham tea industry for my own interest.

Having once started, my early endeavours were brought to the notice of the company who gave me the encouragement I needed to press on.

I threw myself into the project with renewed enthusiasm in the knowledge that the result of my efforts was destined to reach a wider audience.

As can be seen from the list of acknowledgements, I made myself a nuisance to many people, all of whom, I am pleased to say, were most co-operative and interested in my subject, which made my task that much easier.

While tea continues to be drunk the world over there will be a story to tell. I feel privileged to have written the history of 'Typhoo' and the Birmingham tea industry.

K. J. Williams
Sutton Coldfield, 1989

ACKNOWLEDGEMENTS

WITHOUT the help of so many people and organisations this book could not have been written and it is to them I would like to express my appreciation.

To those former 'Typhoo' employees who so patiently withstood my questioning, Edith Carey, Ellen Corbett, Christina Fryer, Clara Edith Aulton (*née* Simister), Edith Shutt (*née* Grainger), E. H. Pedvin, A. J. Pendry and F. Parkin. Their personal reminscences provided an insight into the early days of 'Typhoo' and of its founder Sir John Sumner.

John Black Sumner, the founder's grandson, produced some superb family photographs and Mr J. N. Jones, secretary to the Sir John Sumner Trust, came up with a vital Sumner name.

I am grateful to Eric Tye for his encouragement and also his knowledge of the Priory Tea Co. Pat Jennings for her assistance in locating past 'Typhoo' employees. Pat Wilson for use of her 'Typhoo' newscuttings scrapbook. Jean Tovey for the History Penknife story. David Grieg for the Melrose Royal Visit photographs. Chris Henderson for his Kardomah information, Judi Camp and Keith England for their advertising pictures.

For the ration book I am indebted to Miss E. V. M. James. To my mother for her happy valley memories, but who has sadly died before publication. My wife Maureen, whom I met at 'Typhoo', who helped with stories of the 1950s. Eric Miller of Coleshill Civic Society for Sumner's Coleshill High Street shop photograph. W. A. Camwell for the war damaged tram photograph. Douglas V. Jones for a rare Cadbury print and Phillip S. Wells for his Liverpool docks photograph.

If it wasn't for reference libraries, museums and private collections the task for historians would be almost impossible. As I was required to spend much time in quiet solitude in such establishments, to them I must now extend my thanks.

Joe Mackenna and the staff of the Birmingham Reference Library who were very kind and helpful with my requests for old records, books and particularly for organising the reproduction of old pictures and material. The staff of Sutton Reference Library for use of their facilities and access to the many old record books. John Crompton, Keeper of Social and Industrial History of the Black Country Museum for the photograph of 'Typhoo's' first tram advertising. Birmingham Assay Office for the Boulton and Fothergill Silver Tea Pot photograph. Nicholas Molyneux, of Birmingham Museum and Art Gallery, for photographing the Priory Stone. Andrew Holliday of Walsall Local History Centre for Walsall Priory Tea advertisement. *Birmingham Post & Mail* for old material and the Lewis Williams cartoon. Marion Peters, Coleshill Library, for Sumner's Coleshill advertisements. Helen Davies, Cadbury Archives, for locating those dusty files. The Opie Museum for the earliest 'Typhoo' packet and Anita Crocker, Ceylon Tea Centre, for her slides.

My thanks go to Derek Reid for his encouragement and support for the whole project and Paul Rigg whose personal involvement and organisation skills were invaluable.

Eva Smith who was able to decipher my ramblings and to all at Quiller Press – Jeremy Greenwood, Hugh Tempest-Radford and Hugo Frost – whose combined efforts presented a publication which is a recommendation in itself.

To my wife Maureen for waiting for those odd jobs in the house to be done whilst I indulged in researching and writing this book.

And finally my apologies to anyone I may have inadvertently missed out.

TY·PHOO

1. From the Bush to the Bull Ring

THE plant *Camellia sinensis* is a familiar one to botanists; the general public know it better by its more common name of tea. Its cultivation can be traced back to China in the fourth century AD where it had a medicinal reputation which persisted until the twentieth century and acted as an aid to sales. It is in China that we find the first book published about tea; *Ch'a Ching* was commissioned by a group of merchants in the year 780 and written by Lu Yu. The earliest record of an Englishman to mention tea in writing is in 1615 when R. Wickham, an agent of the East India Tea Company, whilst living on the Japanese island of Hirade, wrote to a friend in Macao asking him to send a pot of 'the best sort of chaw'.

Although tea had already reached Europe in the sixteenth century, it took another hundred years before it became generally

Samuel Pepys, the famous diarist, drank his first cup of tea in London on 25 September 1660 and this he recorded in his diary:
And afterwards did send for a Cupp of Tee (a China drink) of which I have never drank before.

THE BULL RING
BIRMINGHAM,
SHAMBLES AND MARKET CROSS
1750

KJWilliams

At the beginning of the eighteenth century, the Bull Ring was occupied by a number of butchers' shops known as the Shambles. Up the hill was the Old Cross, the upper rooms of which served as a courtroom. Shops and houses flanked the Bull Ring which was named after the bull-baiting that took place there. St Martin's Church stood on the site of an earlier church dating back to the twelfth century.

In 1769 an Act of Parliament was obtained granting the Birmingham authorities permission to remove the Shambles and Market Cross. This would effectively turn the Bull Ring into a large triangular open space allowing more traders into the outside market. The removal of the Market Cross, however, did not take place until 1784; until that time its upper rooms were used by the Commissioners of the Court of Requests.

accepted. During those early days of tea importation the main area of tea drinking was in the London area, promoted through the many coffee houses that spread around the capital. It was an expensive commodity; Thomas Garraway, the proprietor of a well-known London coffee house, refers to the price of his tea as ranging from 16 to 60 shillings per pound – a vast sum at the time. If the tea had reached Birmingham in those early days its price certainly would have put it beyond the reach of the ordinary man. In 1650 Birmingham was a small town with a population of about 5,500 persons, dispersed amongst 15 streets and 900 houses. Fifty years later the population had tripled; there were 28 streets and 2,504 houses. The Bull Ring lay above the River Rea and the moated manor house of the De-Bermingham family and was where the ancient market was held. It was in the grocers' premises in and around the Bull Ring that the Birmingham tea business began.

The claims for the medicinal properties of Dr Stoughton's Elixir were mild compared with those appearing in an advertisement for Desault's Grand Specific Antivene on 27 September 1742. Again needing to be taken with tea or other liquids, this claimed cures which, until the arrival of modern drugs, would have been nothing short of miraculous.

Confirmation that tea drinking was becoming more common in Birmingham was shown by an advertisement in Aris's *Birmingham Gazette or General Correspondent*, dated 24 May 1742, in which Benjamin Mansell, whose tea warehouse was just

This advertisement appeared in Thomas Aris's 'Birmingham Gazette' on 4 January 1742, and is the earliest reference to tea in Birmingham.

Thomas Aris obtained much of the information he used in reporting on political events from coffee houses – mostly in London. These were regular meeting places for the business fraternity and sold not only coffee but also cocoa and tea.

The manor house of the De-Bermingham family in 1814.

below the Bull Ring in Edgbaston Street, offered fine teas on wholesale terms and a discount to any chapman who layed out five pounds or more.

Canal or rail transport was not then available, so supplies obtained from his London warehouse would have been conveyed by road to Birmingham. Roads in those days left a lot to be desired and the journey to and from London would have been slow, hazardous and not without incident. *Aris's Gazette* of Monday, 18 October 1742 reported the following story:

Last week Mr Frederick Bull, an eminent Tea-Merchant in Cornhill coming from Wolverhampton in Staffordshire to London was overtaken on the road by a single man on horseback, whom he took for a Gentleman; but after they had rode three or four miles together the man ordered him to deliver, which Mr. Bull took to be in jest; but he told him he was in earnest, and accordingly robb'd him of about four Guineas and his watch, and

3

afterwards rode with him three miles till they came near a town, when the Highwayman rode off.

Evidently the experience did not put Frederick Bull off the Midlands for, only three months later, we read in the *Gazette* that he had joined Benjamin Mansel in business.

BY FREDERICK BULL AND BENJAMIN MANSEL
OF LONDON
AT THEIR WAREHOUSE IN EDGBASTON STREET
BIRMINGHAM
ARE SOLD ALL SORTS OF FINE TEAS, COFFEES AND
CHOCOLATE, WHOLESALE AT THE SAME PRICE AS
THEIR WAREHOUSE IN LONDON.

The latter's name had now dropped the second 'l', only to recover it again in Sketchley's *Birmingham Directory* of 1767 which records that the tea warehouse of B. Mansell – the only one listed – had moved from Edgbaston Street to 28 High Street, a more prominent position in town.

The partnership between Mr Mansel and Mr Bull does not seem to have lasted very long for an advertisement in the *Gazette* dated April 1744 refers to Benjamin Mansel and Company of London and their warehouse in Edgbaston Street – but makes no mention of Mr Bull.

It would appear that in 1743 Mr Mansel had some competition in the town as far as tea sales were concerned for an announcement in the *Gazette* on Monday, 26 September 1743 informed the citizens of Birmingham that there was to be sold at reasonable rates at Mrs Balmers over against the Angel and Hen and Chickens in the High Street, Birmingham, 'a fresh quantity of lemons and oranges, likewise fine teas, coffee, chocolate and Scotch Snuff as cheap as any one in Town, Wholesale or Retail.'

In the mid-eighteenth century a heavy import duty was imposed on tea, raising the price to between 6 and 20 shillings per pound and resulting in tea being added to the list of goods thought worth smuggling into the country. Concerned at the poor return on their trade, the grocers in Birmingham decided to make some cut-backs to rectify the situation. In November 1760, together with their counterparts in Kidderminster, Stourbridge and Wolverhampton, they inserted an advertisement in the local press which ran for a few weeks prior to Christmas:

> The Grocers, Druggists, Tea-Sellers &c. in Birmingham give this notice to their customers that they have all unanimously agreed to leave off the custom of giving Christmas boxes for the future and hope it will not be took amiss, as the profits of grocery and tea in general are so much reduced, they will not admit of it.

In spite of their combined efforts they did not succeed and the

Dr Samuel Johnson was a regular visitor to Birmingham during the eighteenth century. A self-confessed 'hardened and shameless tea drinker', he was, according to 'The Life of Dr Johnson' (first published in 1791): 'A gross feeder but for most of his life did not drink wine; he could abstain but could not be temperate, and drank prodigious quantities of tea, with which he cheered himself in the morning, and solaced himself in the evening.'

Johnson's own description of tea was: 'TEA.n.f. [a word, I suppose, Chinese; thé, Fr] a Chinese plant, of which the infusion has lately been much drunk in Europe.'

John Wesley, the Methodist preacher, was a frequent visitor to Birmingham. In his early days he was strongly opposed to the drinking of tea, considering it a serious risk to health.

In later years, however, he was converted to the pleasures of taking tea and saw in tea an aid for his temperance drive. In 1761, Josiah Wedgwood made for him a giant teapot capable of holding a gallon of liquid and decorated with pictures of Wesley and some of his ministers.

practice continued.

Perhaps the greatest inhibitor as far as tea sales were concerned was the large consumption of alcoholic drinks. Sketchley's *Birmingham Directory* of 1767 shows just how great was the opposition: it lists only one tea warehouse (Mansell's) and fifty grocers in the town as against 295 publicans.

It was at this time that a number of public tea gardens opened on the outskirts of Birmingham. Looking back to the eighteenth century, R. K. Dent wrote in 1894 in *The Making of Birmingham*:

> There were few indeed of the suburban taverns which did not boast a tea garden where a few arbours, a few flowers and shrubs and a supply of tea and other (stronger) liquids afforded sufficient attraction to the artisan and his family on the rare occasions on which they could leave the close court and the ill-ventilated workshop for such rural delight as the suburban tea gardens afforded.

We find one such tavern, The Anchor, being advertised for letting in *Aris's Gazette* in 1798.

The Aston Cross Tavern opened as a licensed house and tea garden in 1795; when the first landlord, Mr Barron, died his widow kept it on and ran it until her death in 1817. The Spring Gardens served tea to the public until 31 July 1801, whilst the

Built in the eighteenth century, the Angel Inn on the Stratford Road was then a coach-ride out of town and boasted a fine tea garden. This engraving shows an old stage coach which had passed through the toll-bar on the Stratford Road; also visible is the side-bar at the entrance to Ladypool Lane. (From R. K. Dent's, 'The Making of Birmingham', 1894.)

Apollo Tea Gardens survived until 1840 and the Beach Gardens until 1854. Vauxhall Gardens, with its lawns, flower beds, arbours and fountains, provided another popular place of amusement for the citizens of Birmingham during the eighteenth century. Its programme of events included Public Tea Days such as the one which took place on 2 July 1781.

Having served the community for many years, Vauxhall Gardens fell to speculative builders, together with the old manor

The Apollo Hotel and Tea Garden, on the banks of the River Rea, Moseley Street.

Birmingham, Vaux-Hall, 2d July, 1781.

La Danſe en le Jardin.

A. PEMBERTON reſpectfully acquaints his Friends and the Public, That on Thurſday next, the 5th of July, will be

A PUBLIC TEA DAY.

A Band of Muſic is provided for the Dance. The Door will be opened at Three o'Clock---the Muſic begin at Four. Admittance One Shilling, for which a Sixpenny Ticket will be delivered that will be received in the Houſe for its Value, upon the above Day.

☞ A cold Collation, as uſual upon Concert Nights.

Advertisement from the 'Gazette', 2 July 1781.

house of the Holte family. The estate was carved up into streets and now lies covered with bricks, mortar and concrete.

Some Birmingham manufacturers were able to take advantage of the tea trade by producing articles connected with it. We know, for instance, that a Mr Ford ran a tea and coffee urn manufacturing business at 23 New Street. We also find japanned tea ware articles popular – ranged from tea tables to waiters' trays, and from baskets to tea chests. A prominent figure amongst the japanners was the printer John Baskerville of Easy Hill. One of his early apprentices, Henry Clay, was to patent a superior form of papier mâché in 1772, and proceed to apply this hardy material to numerous uses, including tea caddies, tea trays and tables. At one time his factory in Newhall Street employed 300 people. Birmingham Toy Makers (makers of trinkets) in the eighteenth century also had a hand in manu-

When Mathew Boulton set up his silver manufactury at Soho, it was then in Staffordshire. Having gained an unrivalled reputation for quality, he attracted around him some very gifted men, such as James Watt of steam engine fame and William Murdoch, the pioneer in gas lighting.

It was through Boulton's persistence that Birmingham obtained its own Assay Office in 1773; he was the first to have his articles assayed and marked in September of that year. Amongst those articles submitted were many relating to tea and its uses: spoons, tea tongs, tea vases, sugar dishes and teapots such as the one illustrated here.

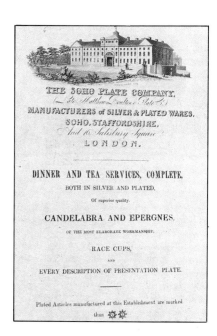

Boulton's factory was still going strong in the middle of the nineteenth century.

facturing articles related to tea, in particular, decorated 'tea chests'; which we know better as tea caddies.

The expansion of the canal network into Birmingham and the Black Country in the second half of the eighteenth century contributed greatly to the growth of the manufacturing industry of the region and the rapid growth of Birmingham and its population. Business competition thrived. We hear of the rivalry between Messrs Durnall and Blunt and Wells: Mr Durnall, brazier and tin-plate worker, of the Tea Urn and Candlestick Warehouse, 49 High Street, near the Welch Cross, Dale End, advertised the sale of his Dutch tea urns and block tin-plate kitchen furniture at the lowest terms being 'the real manufacturer'. Messrs Blunt and Wells retaliated with the following:

A card to Mr Durnall, Brass Candlestick Maker – Blunt and Wells, Lovers of Truth and Enemies to Puffing, present their compliments and would be extremely glad to know where his Real Manufactury of Dutch Tea Urns, Coffee-Pots, Pewter Plates and Dishes &c. &c. &c. is carried on, having never had the pleasure of seeing it: As to his new Boasted Method of Making Block Tin Kitchen Furniture, they are well convinced, may be made at most Tin Plate Workers in town; for it is well known amongst the trade that his present workmen are not superior to other people's but we believe upon trial would be found inferior to many.

There was also competition amongst the town's coffee houses. In 1760 John Freeth – popularly known as Poet Freeth because of his ability to write poetry at the drop of a hat – set up his coffee house in Bell Street off the Bull Ring. *The New Birmingham Directory* for the years 1774 to 1781 shows that Widow Aston was running a coffee house in Cherry Orchard adjacent to Temple Row; and in 1781 Job Overton opened his establishment at 76 High Street.

By 1777 Benjamin Mansell had also lost his monopoly as tea dealer; two new names appear in *The Birmingham Directory* – Joseph Farror of number 7 and Samuel Brooks of 77 High Street. By 1797 Pye's *Birmingham Directory* lists four additional names who acted as tea dealers and grocers: Thomas Bell of Church Street, Edward Bratt of Swallow Street, Thomas Marston of Digbeth and Thomas Walcot of High Street. Joseph Farror went on to extend his business interests and set up a warehouse at 38 Bull Ring for a variety of provisions including his tea. He was prone to advertise in verse and the example (right) appeared on 25 September 1786:

William Hutton, who was to write the first history of Birmingham in 1782, was chosen in 1772 as a Commissioner for the Court of Requests. He was an enthusiastic tea drinker and kept fine green tea as well as common tea at home.

Hutton first visited Birmingham as a runaway apprentice from his native Derby, was impressed and returned in 1750 to open a bookshop in the High Street. The following year he set up the first circulating library and, in 1756, the first paper warehouse. He became very wealthy and entertained many notable people at his house for tea, including Joseph Priestley, the discoverer of oxygen.

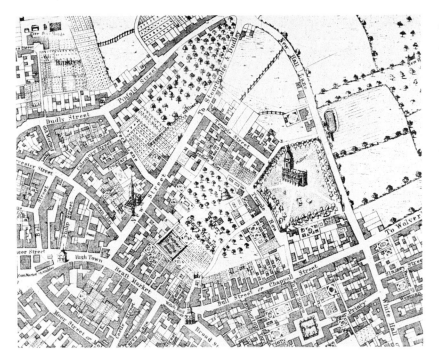

Birmingham, Sept. 25, 1786.
ADVERTISEMENT.
Fine Teas, China-ware, and Glass of the best,
Coffee, Chocolate, and Cocoa, that will stand the Test,
Stone Blue, Poland Starch, and Rice Caroline,
New Mustard Flour, best, second, and fine :
All Kinds of Spices, neat as imported,
Moist, Powder, and Lump Sugars, properly sorted ;
Turkey Figs, new Currants, and Raisins o'th'Sun,
Also Malagas, Prunes, and curious French Plumb :
Blacking Balls, the best of any in Town,
W. P. for to play at Laugh and Lie Down ;
With many more Articles, I wish you to know,
May be bought of J. FARROR, on Terms very low :
His Warehouse in Bull-Ring is No. Thirty-eight,
And Shop to sell Retail is in Temple-street.
Auctioneering perform'd, we* take Leave for to mention,
To insure† your Property I beg your Attention.
* In Partnership with W. Goode, No. 11, New-street.
† Agent to the Phœnix Fire-Office, Lombard-street, London.

This eighteenth century map of Birmingham shows the cherry orchard where widow Aston's coffee house would be sited.

The attractions of a new stopping-off place for tea on the River Rea were loudly acclaimed, as seen in this advertisement on 12 March 1787.

Catherine Hutton.

A note in the 'Gazette' on August 7, 1784 announcing the Old Cross in the Bull Ring was to be pulled down.

By the River Rea.

A decision was made on the 21 July 1784 at a Towns Meeting held in the Public Office, Dale End, that the Old Cross, which was in a ruinous state, was to be pulled down. All the furniture belonging to the Commissioners of the Court of Requests was sold by auction on 13 August 1784, and the Court moved into new premises – an old tea warehouse at 28 High Street. They evidently only occupied part of the building, for Pye's 1797 *Birmingham Directory* shows Mansell still operating his tea warehouse at that address. A century later the premises were known as The Old Court Tea Warehouses.

As supply increased to keep pace with demand, tea became more securely established as a drink associated with leisure and social life. Catherine Hutton, daughter of the historian William Hutton, wrote in 1819 of summer activities in Birmingham:

> For the entertainment of Summer exclusive of the Theatre, there are five Bowling Greens where Gentlemen are amused with their Bowls and the Ladies with their tea.

In addition, there would be visits to tea gardens attached to taverns or trips on the river with refreshments taken at the tea gardens on the riverside. Such boat trips had their rewards as described in Gill's *History of Birmingham*:

> There were fine gardens too, belonging to houses on Spiceal Street and Floodgate Street. The 'lively tripping Rea' added to the rural attraction of Birmingham and boats could be hired by Deritend Bridge to take parties up to pleasant tea gardens beside the river.

TY·PHOO

2. Tea Parties and Rhymes

BY the start of the new century Birmingham's population had risen to 73,670. This growth in population was matched by an increase in the consumption of tea. Tea was being served in inns and coffee houses, as well as in the many public tea gardens to be found on the outskirts of town. Consumption in the home also increased – to the point where, by 1812, tea dealers in Birmingham numbered over twenty-five, according to Thompson & Wrightson's *Triennial Directory*.

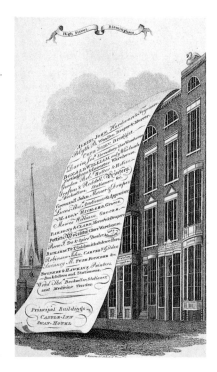

Adams, James	Grocer and tea dealer, Church Street
Barnes, Jeremia	Grocer and tea dealer, Digbeth
Chellingworth, Thomas	Grocer and tea dealer, Coleshill Street
Freer, Thomas	Druggist, tea dealer and oilman, Dale End
Hedges, Thomas	Wholesale grocer and tea dealer, Dale End
Ingram, Henry	Grocer and tea dealer, Bell Street
King, Thomas	Grocer, tea dealer and chandler, High Street
Lea, William	Grocer and tea dealer, High Street
Lefevre, Samuel	Tea dealer, grocer, tallow chandler, bacon and salt butter factor, High Street
Massey, Robert	Tea warehouse, Edmund Street
Maund, James & Co	Tea dealers, Digbeth
Maund, Richard	Grocer and tea dealer, Spiceal Street
Mewis, James	Grocer and tea dealer, High Street
Mewis, William	Grocer and tea dealer, High Street
Moore, Ann	Grocer and tea dealer, Bull Ring
Newton, Joseph	Grocer and tea dealer, Church Street
Oldfield, Thomas	Grocer, tea dealer and oilman, High Street, Deritend
Pountney, Humphrey	Grocer and tea dealer, Digbeth
Pratchett & Noble	Druggists and tea dealers, 97 High Street
Reece, John	Grocer and tea dealer, High Street

J. Bisset's 'Magnificent Directory' of 1808 lists the businesses at a number of buildings in the High Street. The illustration here shows the tea warehouse of Mansell – the earliest name associated with selling tea in Birmingham – has changed hands, to be replaced by J. Reece, 'Tea & Spice Dealer'. Whilst behind is the business of Pratchett & Noble which was sold to William Sumner in 1820.

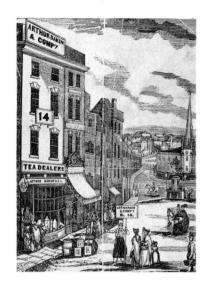

Tea dealers made good use of the publicity methods available at the time. This advertising card c. 1829 was put out by Arthur Dakin and Thomas Ridgway who were partners at 14 Bull Ring until they were declared insolvent in 1833.

Ridgway returned to London and, in 1836, set himself up in King William Street where his business prospered. He later paid off his Birmingham creditors who, in appreciation of such honourable conduct, presented him with an ornate tea service which remains in the Ridgways' boardroom to this day.

The company Thomas Ridgway started has operated successfully ever since in the premium and speciality sectors of the tea market and, since 1987, forms part of Premier Brands (UK) Ltd.

Sherratt, John	Grocer and tea dealer, Coleshill Street
Stubbs, Francis	Grocer and tea dealer, Deritend
Swann, John	Grocer and tea dealer, Snow Hill
Thompson & Watson	Grocers and tea dealers, High Street
Underhill, John	Tea and paper warehouse, Cherry Street
Wills, William	Grocer and tea dealer, High Street
Wood, Samuel	Grocer and tea dealer, etc, Deritend
Wright, Edward	Grocer and tea dealer, wholesale and retail, Bull Street

The increasing popularity of tea spawned a variety of associated trades; water sellers flourished and the *Triennial Directory* lists several manufacturers of such metal articles as Britannia tea bells, teaspoons, teapots and tea kettles. Ornate solid silver tea kettles could only be afforded by the rich, but the perfecting of the process of electro-plating in 1842 – by the Birmingham firm of H. & G. R. Elkington and their associates, Alexander Parkes and Dr John Wright – brought attractive silver-plated utensils within the reach of many more tea drinkers.

The consumption of tea was actively encouraged by the Temperance Movement in its fight against alcohol. Tea would be served at fundraising and recruiting meetings; at one such occasion in Birmingham it is recorded that tea for 250 people was prepared by pouring boiling water on quarter-pound bags of tea placed inside a large, 1 ft deep tin measuring 3 ft by 3 ft. The tea was then sold at the considerable sum of 9*d* for adults and 2½*d* for youths.

Oakley Bennett, tea dealers, had premises at 31 High Street.

Bull Ring, c. 1829
The removal of The Shambles and the Market Cross had left greater space for the open market and had enabled Birmingham in 1809 to be the first city to erect a statue to Nelson there.

One of the founders of the Birmingham Auxiliary Temperance Society was John Cadbury. Born in 1800, at the age of sixteen he had been apprenticed to a tea dealer friend of his father, a John Curdworth of Broadhead & Curdworth at Bridgate, Leeds. Six years later he had gone to London for a year with the firm of Sanderson & Fox in order to gain further experience in the tea trade. He subsequently returned to Birmingham and, in 1824, set up as tea dealer and coffee roaster at 93 Bull Street on capital subscribed by his father, Richard Tapper Cadbury. He, too, operated from Bull Street, having started up there as a draper on his arrival in Birmingham in 1794.

February 1833 saw the laying of the first stone of the new market hall in the Bull Ring. When completed, it measured 365 ft in length and 108 ft in width; an addition to the original design allowed for extensive retail premises to front the Bull Ring, including that of Hodgkins, grocer and tea dealer.

By 1831 John Cadbury had begun to manufacture cocoa and chocolate, first from a warehouse in Crooked Lane, then from Bridge Street. Tea, however, continued to form the predominant part of his business until the early 1870s, some forty years after he had brought in his two sons, Richard and George, to revitalise the declining trade at Bridge Street. As late as 1863, in fact, business there had been so bad that George had contemplated becoming a tea planter in the Himalayas instead. However, turnover suddenly began to improve and, although stock-taking at Bridge Street in 1872 showed that Cadbury's still had an interest in tea, by 1873 this had been emphatically overtaken by the chocolate and cocoa side of the business.

For other people, however, tea continued to be a going concern. Retail outlets in Birmingham and its neighbourhood maintained a steady growth; Pigot & Co.'s *Directory of Warwickshire* for 1835 lists five tea dealers for Sutton Coldfield alone. By 1862, according to the *Business Directory of Birmingham*, the area's considerable number of tea retailers were being served by seven wholesale dealers:

Averill & Smith	139 Digbeth
Brooke Brothers	57 High Street, Bull Ring

Cadbury's premises in 1840.

Slater's 'Directory of Birmingham' for 1852–53 shows that John Cadbury's original premises were taken over by his nephew, Richard Cadbury Barrow, trading as Richard Barrow & Co. This was the forerunner of the Barrow's Stores which were to become so familiar to generations of Birmingham residents and which, in the 1960s, became part of Fitch Lovell's Key Markets division.

The advertising card of Andrews, 'Tea Dealer', who took over the business of Dakin & Co. at 14 Bull Ring.

JOHN CADBURY'S SHOP BULL STREET BIRMINGHAM IN THE EIGHTEEN-THIRTIES

Cadbury Brothers	Bridge Street, Broad Street and 148½ Fenchurch Street, London
Knight, George B.	85 Parade
Lampart & Co.	York Passage, High Street, Bull Ring
Nutter Brothers & Clarke	12 Union Passage
Picken, Edwin	16 Prospect Row

At this time four tea urn makers were working in the city:

Potter, Samuel	187 Hospital Street
Soutter, William	10 New Market Street
Spurrier, William	5 Newhall Street
Stirk, Emanuel	47 Price Street

John Cadbury was aware from the beginning of the commercial value of good publicity. His first advertisement on setting up as tea dealer at 93 Bull Street appeared in Aris's 'Birmingham Gazette' on 1 March 1824; his efforts to attract business also included employing a Chinaman dressed in full native costume to preside over the tea weighing and packing.

And the tea being brewed in those urns was still coming mainly from China, although it would soon be facing serious rivalry from India and Ceylon. The climate in Assam suited the cultivation of *Camellia sinensis* and tea from India gradually came to compete with that from China. The situation was further affected by the devastation of Ceylon's main cash crop, coffee, through an outbreak of the coffee-rust disease. When the island's ruined plantations were reseeded with tea, it could hardly be foreseen that, in twenty years, those seedlings would be responsible for some 15 million lbs of tea being imported into Britain.

Meanwhile, in and around Victorian Birmingham, China tea was still going strong. It was also becoming a more affordable commodity; a pound of Congou seems to have cost around

The 'Ariel' and 'Taeping' were joint winners of the great race of 1866 to bring home to London the first China tea of the season; the premium of ten shillings a ton and the special price of £100 was divided between them.

2 shillings. The 'Grocery and Provision Establishment' of J. T. Hammblett of Sutton Coldfield advertised on 1 January 1870:

Good Congou	1s 4d,
Strong Congou	2s,
Choice Flavoured	2s 6d,
Extra Strong	3s.

In the same newspaper, *The Sutton Coldfield & Erdington News*, S. Ingram & Son offered their 'fine new Congou tea' at 2s and 3s. John Collett & Co. – established in Moor Street in 1863 – advertised in 1871:

> The best and cheapest teas in the United Kingdom. Twelve pounds of sterling breakfast Congou, and six pounds of drawing room tea sent free by rail, on receipt of a Post Office Order for two pounds.

In the same year, the firm of London Star Teas of 74b Worcester Street was selling 2 lbs of its tea at 5s, 3 lbs at 7s 6d and 6 lb at 14s. It also offered 'lock cannisters' in 2-, 3- and 6-lb sizes at 1s 3d, 1s 6d and 2s respectively.

The supply of tea had been greatly facilitated by the opening of the Suez Canal in 1869. Until then, British and American clippers had competed fiercely in the race to bring home the highly valued first teas of the season. The two newly created bunkering stations at Port Said and Aden now allowed steam ships to become economically viable by releasing for cargo some of the space on board which, until then, had been taken up with coal. In addition, the steamers could now complete the round trip to China in 120 days – practically half the time taken by clippers – and so two or three trips a year became feasible. The age of steam had arrived and its consequences on the tea trade were widely felt.

In spite of ever widening consumption of tea during the nineteenth century, sometimes supply outstripped demand. A lecture on a novel way of disposing of excess tea addressed by a Dr Thudichum to the Society of Arts, Birmingham, was reported on 8 January 1870 in the *Sutton and Erdington News*. It consisted of making wine from surplus teas and examples of Dr Thudichums experiments with various China Teas and containing 9 per cent alcohol were made available for members' approval.

Dr Thudichum's scheme does not seem to have taken off to any extent and tea wine never came to rival the other alcoholic beverages dispensed in Birmingham's inns and taverns. In the 1840s there were 995 public houses in the town and, although some tea gardens in the suburbs continued to attract customers, others were coming to the end of their day. The Apollo Tea Gardens closed in 1846, with the Beeches Gardens following suit nine years later. In his *Old and New Birmingham*, published in 1880, R. K. Dent applauds the enterprise of the Birmingham

Although based in Birmingham, Sheaff & Holden also advertised their new season's tea in neighbouring Sutton Coldfield.

The Hen and Chickens, New Street.

The above report by the Public Analyst for Warwickshire was included by R. L. & J. L. Lodge, Tea Merchants, in advertisements for their Dietetic Tea in 1888. The health-promoting claims proved to be good selling points.

Based at 168/9 Broad Street, Lodges sold their Dietetic Tea in 2-lb tins at 2s 4d per pound; 1-lb tins could be sent to customers in all parts of the UK on receipt of postage stamps or postal orders to the value of 2s 7d.

Coffee House Company Ltd. in the 1870s in catering for the artisan population of the town by establishing handsome coffee houses in all the principal thoroughfares. These sold not only coffee, but also tea, milk and cocoa at very reasonable prices and adopted every means to become a counter-attraction to public houses and gin palaces.

Tea was considered a desirable drink for children, too. George Cadbury often arranged tea parties for children of the poor at his home 'Woodbrooke'; in 1881 he had a large tent put up in a field by Woodbrooke Farm and here water was boiled and milk, tea and sugar supplied for the children who had been brought from schools in Birmingham. Later he built 'the Barn' in which he could seat 700 people – frequently including children – at his organised tea parties.

It was not only individuals who held tea parties. The first of the Chapel 'Tea Fights' – great social gatherings – took place in 1815 and tea continued to be a favourite beverage at political meetings of all persuasions. The Chartists took tea at their 1841 Christmas celebration in Birmingham Town Hall and, two years later, on 22 January 1843, some 1700 supporters attended the Anti-Corn Law League tea party – including the prominent reformist, John Bright, who later became MP for Birmingham.

By this time the supply of water for domestic use had begun to be eased. Walter Showell's *Dictionary of Birmingham* – published in 1885 – describes one of the old water pumps:

> The Old Cock Pump was formerly under St Martin's Church-yard Wall, from which the Water-Carriers and others obtained their supply of Drinking Water. Many of us can recollect the old Digbeth men, with their shoulder-yoke and two buckets, plodding along to find customers for their 'Wartâ', certain elderly ladies are still in existence who would fear the shortening of their lives, were their tea kettles filled with aught but pure Digbeth water, though it does not come from the pump at St Martin's, for that was removed in 1873.

The handle of the old Cock Pump had been taken by a blacksmith who had found himself short of metal, to be remade into a horseshoe.

Allison Street provided another source of water; it was here, in 1854, that Mr Clark of Maida Hill, London, successfully bored an artesian well which allowed for 72,000 gallons of water to be pumped out every day. The *Weekly Post* of the time writes:

> A showily painted cart may still be seen in the streets of Birmingham dispensing the Digbeth water which was so famous and so popular till about fifty years ago. The supply sold comes from an Artesian Well bored in or near Well Street out of Allison Street. There were several Private Wells in Digbeth, especially on the

Taken around 1905 in Walsall, this photograph shows a large Priory Tea billboard on the corner of Peal Street. On the left is the delicensed Shakespeare Inn, the cellars of which led into ancient limestone caverns, cutting deep into Church Hill.

East side near the corner of Park Street. Until recently two or three pumps supplied the ever welcome water for general use and especially for tea.

But it was not until the end of the nineteenth century that the reservoirs created in the Elan Valley in Wales by the Birmingham Corporation secured for the city a regular supply of water on tap.

The last quarter of the century proved to be as busy as ever on the Birmingham tea scene. Established businesses were on the move, merging, expanding or folding, new firms were setting up – and all the while hoardings vied with other methods of publicity in the competition to promote one brand of tea or another.

One of Birmingham's last steam trams –
photographed at King's Heath in 1906 –
bore a large advertisement for Priory
Tea. The old track was replaced by rails
for the electric tram which officially took
over on 1 January 1907.

A song on the lips of many at the time celebrated the virtues of 'A Cup of Tea':

> Some there are who seeking pleasure
> Mix themselves some eau-de-vie,
> Whisky, rum or old Geneva
> But when I'm low, I take to tea.

CHORUS

> Celebrate in song, Pekoe or Souchong,
> Morning Congo, too, syrupy Foo Shoo,
> But give me, oh give to me
> A full and fragrant cup of tea.

Another song of the time started with the line 'Lewises Beautiful Tea'; this marked the setting-up of their own tea warehouse by Lewises, whose tea had gone on sale at 2s per pound. Lewises had already had a successful department store in Manchester when, in 1885, they had built their Birmingham store on the corner of Corporation Street and Bull Street – in the busiest part of town.

Songs, however, were not always complimentary; tea consumers were quite capable of judging the quality of the products on offer. A correspondent in the *Birmingham Weekly Post* in 1933 recalled that the Bombay Co. – which operated from the High

Street before 1888 – used to issue coupons to their tea customers to be exchanged for a variety of gifts. Unfortunately the tea was very indifferent and people in the neighbourhood would send their youngsters to collect their weekly supply and vouchers. On the way home from school one boy meeting another would shout the slogan 'Bombay', to be answered with 'Rotton Tay'. The tea cost 2s a pound and the resulting song went like this:

> Beautiful two shilling tea
> Sixpence you pay for the quarter
> Put half a pound into the pot
> It will only just colour the water.

Gifts with purchase promotions were not unusual; imaginative merchandising and advertising campaigns jostled each other in the attempt to sell more tea. No man was more adept in this respect than J. H. Brindley who, in 1893, founded the Priory Tea and Coffee Company. In the effort to ensure that his Priory Tea received maximum publicity, in 1894 he employed Lieut. Lemprière to fly over Birmingham in his balloon in order to drop leaflets. These announced:

PRIORY TEA – BEST VALUE IN THE WORLD

> This handbill was dropped from the
> skies by Lieut. Lemprière, navigating
> The Golden Eagle Balloon
> June 16th 1894

Three years later he was to offer a hundred pianos free to customers as part of his publicity campaign. Priory Tea hoardings were among the first to be fixed onto the sides of steam trams in the town and it was not unusual to hear children in the streets chanting:

> One, two, three,
> Drink Priory Tea

especially when paid a penny by Mr Brindley to do so. Named after the site of the packing warehouse in Lower Priory, Dale End, Priory Tea became very popular and its name and reputation spread further afield.

J. H. Brindley's flair and experience were to be of great assistance to his grocer friend, John Sumner, when the latter came to set up his new business, Sumner's 'Typhoo Tea' Ltd, in 1905.

TY·PHOO

3. Between the Wars

THE chimes of Big Brum heralded in the twentieth century. By now tea was confirmed as the favourite drink of both Birmingham and the whole country, having outstripped ale. Now Britain could truly be called the nation of tea drinkers.

In Birmingham by now there were over sixty tea merchants, according to the lists in Bennett's *Business Directory* and Kelly's *Directory*, and the tea they were selling was mostly of the large leaf variety. Consumption figures for 1903 show that 55 per cent

Birmingham. **Bennett's Business Directory.** Birmingham

TEACHER—WRITING.

Hyde J E, Midland Buildings, New st

TEA MERCHANTS.

Albert Tea Co, Ltd, 34 Winson Green rd
Althams Tea Co. Ltd. 23 High st, Aston
Ashbury C A & Co, 139 High st, Aston
Ashby J & Sons, Castle Street Chambers
Averill & Smith, Cambridge st
Baker W, 160 Mary st, Balsall Heath
Barber & Co. New st, Worcester st and Pershore st
BARROW'S STORES, LTD, tea and coffee merchants, 74, 76 and 78 Corporation st and 93 Bull st—see advt
BLOOMER H, tea merchant, 24 Aitken Chambers, Cannon st. Tel. Add. "Bloomer, B'ham."
BOMBAY TEA CO. LTD., 10, 11 and 12 Moor st. Tel. Add. "Bombay." Tel. No. 1928
Broomhall F, 374 Coventry rd & 237 Highgate rd
Buggett & Co. 24 Lodge rd
Buggett & Co. 7 Great Hampton st
Burnett J H, 10 Quadrant Chambers, New st
Burrow G, 165 Deritend, and 1 Bissell st
Buxton J & Co. 177 High st Aston
Carter & Co. 404 Dudley rd
East India Produce Co, Helena st, Parade ger
Foster T & Co. 58 Bull st
Ginder W L, 73 Ruskin Buildings, Corporation st
Goldstein A. 36 Florence st, Holloway Head
Graham W T, 308 Coventry rd
HASTILOW T & CO, wholesale tea merchants, Gothic Arcade, Snow Hill
Holden G. 175 High st, Aston
Home & Colonial Stores, 71 and 359 Stratford rd, 171a Soho rd, 209 Great Lister st & 117 Broad st
Indian. Ceylon & China Tea Co., 18 Worcester st—J Fitt, manager
Jackson E, Bell Buildings, Bordesley Green
JACKSON G, tea merchant, 100 High st, 103 Corporation st & 49 Bull st—see advt

JEWELL W & CO, wholesale tea and coffee merchants, Bordesley Green
Keen G. 193 Gooch st. Longmore st, 51 Spring Hill, 1 Ledsam st, and 175 Balsall Heath rd
KING S & SON, tea and coffee dealers. 92 Dale End
King S T. 237 Broad st, 17 Spiceal st, 96 Bull st, 1 Deritend Bridge 206 Gooch st, 28 Horse Fair, 40 Great Lister st, 121 Newtown Row. 274 Coventry rd, 123 Summer Lane, 16 Lichfield rd, 142 Stratford rd and 159 Spring Hill
Liptons, Ltd, 74 High st & 244 Gooch st
LODGE R L & J L, tea and coffee merchants. and Italian warehousemen. 168 & 169 Broad st, Islington. Tel. No. 273
Matthews W. 121a Lichfield rd. Aston
Miles H & Co. Scotland Passage
Morris S W, 32 Union st
Murcott A & Co. Helena st
Neale G E. 68 Stratford rd
Neale's Tea Stores, 101 Moor st, 108 Dudley st, 351 Monument rd. 507 Stratford rd. Sparkhill, 204 Ladypool rd, 349 Stratford rd. 392 Lodge rd, 106 Villa rd, Six Ways, Smethwick. 20 Cape Hill, High st. Smethwick. High st, King's Heath, 108 Lichfield rd. High st, Bournbrook, 68 Stratford rd. 45 Spring Hill, 82 Bristol st. 202 Broad st and Bristol rd. Bournbrook
Palmer S, 169 Ladypool rd
Palmer S C, 45 Hallam st
Pearks' Tea and Butter Stores, 151 Stoney Lane, and Moseley Village
PEEK BROS., & WINCH, Ltd, wholesale tea merchants, 6 Quadrant Chambers, New st. Tel. No. 1744. Tel. Address: "Valiant, B'ham."
Phillips T H. 342 Bearwood rd
Poole W, 171 Broad st
Priory Tea & Coffee Co. Ltd., Priory Buildings, Lower Priory
Ragoona Tea Co. 92 Conybere st
Red Trading Stamp Co. 24 Snow Hill
Rickett & Co. 381 Ladypool rd
Ricketts & Co. 251 Brunswick rd
Ridgway & Co. Ltd. 5 Bull st, 68, 70. 72 and 74 Hockley st
ROBERTS B & CO, LTD, tea and coffee merchants, 1 Corporation st
ROXBURGH & CO. wholesale tea and coffee merchants, Old Court House. 28, High st
Scarf T, 144 Berners st
Southern E, 4 Park rd, Aston
Stratford W J 12 Quadrant Chambers. New st
Tregilgas J & Son 211 Newhall st

Tea Merchants—con.

Universal Tea Co. 338 Newtown Row, 19 Lichfield rd, Aston, 67 Spring Hill, 6 Lodge rd, 328 Coventry rd, 147 Stratford rd 1 Nechells Park rd & 80 High st, Bournbrook
Walford F H, 332 Gooch st
Ward T, 210 Edward rd
Warriner & Mason, 97 & 98 Digbeth, 16a Prospect Row, 138 King Edward's rd, Ellen st and Hingeston st
Webster J W, 187 Hagley road Edgbaston
Woodcock P W, 322 Coventry rd
Wright & Marshall, 143 Ladypool rd, Sparkbrook, and 532 Coventry rd, Small Heath

TELEPHONE COMPANY.

National Telephone Co, Head Office, Edmund st

Call Offices :—
Arblaster & Churchill, New st
A J Pattison, New st
Avenue Hotel, Park rd, Aston
Bodega Agency, New st (Café Royal)
Bodega Co, Great Hampton st
Central Restaurant Corporation st
Cobden Hotel. Corporation st
Colonnade Hotel, New st
Crown Inn, New st
Dingley's Hotel, Moor st
Duke of York Hotel, Harborne
Exchange Restaurant, Stephenson Place
F Mealing, 146 Bishop st
Grand Hotel, Colmore Row
Great Western Hotel, Colmore Row
Hare & Hounds, King's Heath
Harborne & Edgbaston Institution, Harborne
H Nixon, King's Heath
Horsefall's, Monument rd
Iron Exchange, Stephenson Place
Jenny Lind, Aston Church rd
J F Rhodes, Bristol st
Lamp, Bull st
Law Courts. Corporation st
Library, Margaret st
Manchester Hotel, Snow Hill
Midland Institute, Paradise st
Newman's. Broad st Corner
,, Corporation st
,, New st
,, Stephenson Place
Old Nelson Inn. Great Lister st
Pig Market, Montague st
Plough & Harrow, Jamaica

TAI—TEA 957

TEA MERCHANTS.

Absolom, Crocker & Co. Seymour st
Albert Tea Co. Lim. 34 Winson Green rd
Barber & Co. 28, 30 & 32 Pershore st. Telephone, 2980 ; Telegrams, "Tea plant"
Barber & Co. Quadrant, 4 Worcester st
Broomhall Francis, 237 Highgate road Sparkbrook
Fitt John & Co. 18 Worcester street
Foster Thomas & Co. 58 Bull street
Freeman Osborne Fras. 27 Charlotte st
Ginder Walter L. Ruskin chambers Corporation street
Hanson S. Son & Barter, Lincoln's inn Corporation street
Hastilow Thos. & Co. 16 Gothic arcade Snow hill
Hindoola Tea Co (The), Lench street
Holden Charles, 175 High street. Aston & 24 Ledsam street
Indian Tea Estates Limited (The (James A. Noinn, manager), 7 Clevedon road, Balsall heath
Infusora Tea Co. Limited, 41 Church st
Koh-i-Noor Tea Co. 8 Gothic arcade Snow hill
Lipton Limited. 244 Gooch street
Liverpool (The) China & India Tea Co. Limited, 42A, New street
Lloyd, Pigott & Co. 2 Corn Exchange passage, High street
Lodge R. L. & J. L. 168 & 169 Broad st
Mazawattee Tea Co. Lim. (H. Rose agent), 4 Corn Exchange passage High street
Miles Henry & Co. (& blenders), Central bldgs. Scotland pas. High st
Miles Joseph Henry (agent), 2 Central buildings, Scotland passage, High st
Neale's Tea Stores, 187 High st. Aston
Priory Tea & Coffee Co. Limited, Lower Priory
Ridgways Limited, 5 Bull street
Roberts Robt. & Co. Lim. 1 Corporation st
Roxburgh & Co. 72 Moor street
Tregilgas John & Son, Cambridge st
Universal Tea Co. 328 Coventry road 338 New Town row ; 67 Spring hill 147 Stratford road ; 1 Nechells Park road & 249 Bearwood hill, Smethwick 19 Lichfield road, Aston & 6 Lodge road, Hockley
Warriner & Mason Limited, 96½, 97 & 98 Digbeth

was tea of Indian origin, 30 per cent came from Ceylon while sales of China tea, which had once had the monopoly of the market, had slumped to a mere 7½ per cent.

Some of the names in Bennett's and Kelly's directories have interesting origins. James Ashby & Sons came from the Quaker partnership of Wilson and Ashby.

Barrow's Stores Ltd took its name from Richard Cadbury Barrow, nephew of John Cadbury, the founder of the Cadbury

A section of Bennett's 'Business Directory' and of Kelly's 'Directory of Birmingham', 1903, showing the tea merchants.

Built in 1902, the Great Western Arcade allowed shoppers to browse under cover. The arcade ran from Corporation Street to Colmore Row and housed several tea-shops. This view towards Temple Row was taken in 1904.

Maypole grocers advertising their own blend of tea.

business whose tea premises in Bull Street Richard had taken over when his uncle John had gone on to pursue his interest in cocoa and chocolate. Barrow's was sold to Key Markets division of Fitch Lovell in the 1960s.

Budgett & Co. may have been quite independent of the Bristol firm of HH&S Budgett who packed and sold Budgett's Golden Blend Tea.

Home and Colonial Stores were started in 1885 by the Drew family in partnership with William Slaughter and John Musker.

Pearks Tea and Butter Stores may well have been connected with the Pearks of South Kensington who underwent great expansion in 1886 after having run a single shop since 1860.

The Peek brothers of Peek Brothers & Winch Ltd originally came from Loddiswell in Devon. Richard had gone to London in around 1800 to work with the tea firm of Sanderson & Barclay and had been followed to the capital ten years later by William. The latter had set up his own business of Peek & Co. which was changed to Peek Bros when the two brothers joined forces. In 1834 William moved to Liverpool where he took a partner called Winch, later opening a branch in London as Peek & Winch. In 1895 the two Peek firms joined together under the name Peek Bros & Winch. It was with Peek & Co. that Arthur Brooke, the founder of Brooke Bond tea, started before setting up his own tea company in Manchester.

The Liverpool, China & India Tea Company was set up in Liverpool in 1868 by two brothers called Vey who had been dealing in tea since 1844. They opened an Exhibition Café where they sold cups of tea and coffee as well as packet tea over the counter. Then came more shops throughout the country retailing various fine blends of tea. Soon their tea was to become a household name: Kardomah Tea. In 1911 The Kardomah Tea Company was at 78 High Street and the Liverpool China & India Tea Co. at 42A New Street. In 1964 they became part of Trusthouse Forte; today they form part of Premier Brands (UK) Ltd, in the same stable as Typhoo Tea Ltd.

D. F. Shillington of Harrison & Crosfields is said to have invented the brand name 'Mazawattee Tea'. It was produced by a company which had been started by John Booth Densham and which later traded as Densham & Sons when he took his

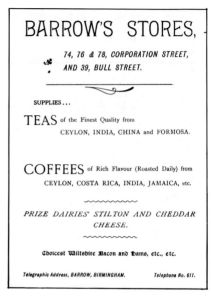

This is the first advertisement to include tea from Formosa. By 1902 Barrow's Stores had a large presence in Corporation Street, occupying numbers 74, 76 and 78.

This advertisement for Barber's Teas was fixed to the wall above a shop in High Street, Harborne, opposite the Green Man in 1941. Barbers was absorbed by Twinings in 1961.

Barber's Teas card from 1958.

four sons into partnership. The company sold out after World War II and is now a subsidiary of Burton Sons & Saunders. The tea itself is no longer on sale. Kelly's 'Directory of Birmingham' for 1908 shows the Mazawattee Tea Company Ltd at 13 High Street, having moved from 4 Corn Exchange Passage. H. Rose is listed as agent.

The outbreak of the First World War in 1914 did not have an immediate effect on the availability of tea but from 1916, as the U-boats affected shipping, queues for goods formed at shops. On 11 December 1916 a Food Controller was appointed. During the first half of 1917 tea was placed on the Import Restrictions Committee's list of luxury foods and drinks, with the result that less than half of the previous half year's total was brought into the country. The following year, however, the Ministry ensured greater supplies although all tea was placed into four price

This picture shows the premises of Roxburgh & Co., tea merchants in The Old Court Tea Warehouse, once occupied by Mansell, Birmingham's first tea merchant.

categories with 90 per cent being price controlled. Despite all the problems, it was not until 1918 that the housewife was required to register with her retailer who received an allocation of 2 oz per customer.

By the end of the war tea outlets in Birmingham had increased considerably. Kelly's *Directory* of 1918 lists more than 850 grocers and tea dealers from whom the general public could obtain regular supplies, in addition to the seventeen tea merchants in the town. One of these was a new firm, the Imperial Tea Company, based at 35 Imperial Buildings, Dale End.

The sale by auction of privately owned tea resumed again on 5 May 1919. Since 1834 these auctions traditionally took place in Mincing Lane, London. One of the first tea merchants to acquire premises there was Robert Major Holborn, whose firm

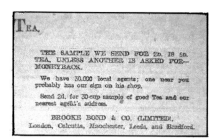

Founded in Manchester in 1869, by 1903 Brooke Bond & Co. Ltd was based in Dunstan's Hill, London and was selling its tea in the Midlands. This Brooke Bond advertisement is from the 'Birmingham Daily Post' of 9 November 1903.

FAULTLESS IN FLAVOUR
RICHNESS AND DIGESTIBILITY

There is no indication in this advertisement – which appeared in the 'Birmingham Gazette & Express' at Christmas 1905 – as to the origins or packer of this tea.

Nor do we know if consumers did come again for another cup of Cum-a-Gen.

Barber & Co. was founded in 1797 in Bishopsgate, London, and, when the London firm went into liquidation, became Barber's Teas of Birmingham dealing exclusively in tea packing.

Brooke Bond expanded fast. It took over the Priory Tea & Coffee Company of Birmingham in 1919 – the year that Mr Brindley, the latter's founder, died.

At Christmas they offered 'Christmas Tea and Cannisters'. Brooke Bond Tea in pretty Cannisters. The cost ½ lb 2d and 6 lb 8d.

of R. M. Holborn & Sons Ltd was founded in 1775. Holborns were taken over in 1936 by the Birmingham tea blenders and packers, Typhoo Tea Ltd; unfortunately, during World War II, Holborns had to be closed down.

Between the two World Wars some Birmingham tea merchants disappeared without trace but, on the other hand, quite a few of those recorded in 1928 were new in the trade. Unfortunately many supplied the barest of information and exist in name only. The Assam & Ceylon Tea Company operated from 41 Hylton Street with the Regent Tea Co. as a close neighbour in Victoria Street, while the Brookfield Tea Company was based at 114 Coopers Lane, Smethwick. Dominion Tea Stores of 95 (back of) Station Street were listed under the heading 'Tea Merchants' while Hurrell's Stores Ltd were selling their tea from two shops at 100 High Street and at 131 Broad Street. The Forward Tea Company could be found at 18 Bright Buildings, 100 John Bright Street. The Northern Counties Tea Co. Ltd was just off Hurst Street, in Ladywell Walk, while the Ombersley Tea Co. were further out of town, at 108D Alcester Road,

Nectar Tea was widely advertised; here its name is displayed on the front of one of the new electric trams at the terminus in Cotteridge in about 1912.

Moseley. Another Moseley tea merchant was Price Golden Tea Company – at 72 Dovey Road.

Priory Tea and Coffee Company Ltd was a genuinely Birmingham firm which was founded in 1893 by J. H. Brindley in Lower Priory.

Ridgway & Co. Ltd started in the Bull Ring as a partnership of Dakin and Ridgway – which did not prosper. However, in 1836 Thomas Ridgway set up a more successful business in King William Street, London.

At 20 Castle Street in 1928 could be found the Sovereign Tea Company; this was then a narrow street between Marks & Spencer and the old Birmingham Co-operative Society building in the High Street. Access into Castle Street is now restricted by redevelopment but, although it only runs a few yards, the nameplate is still affixed to the wall of the new building. It was in Castle Street in the early 1900s that, having moved from 25–26 High Street, the newly formed Sumner's 'Typhoo' Tea Ltd set up its packing operation.

Sturgess Sheldon & Sons were at 55 Carlton House, 28 High Street, while a short distance away, in Coleshill Street, which today is contiguous with Aston University, was Townsend &

Happy Valley, Yardley Wood, c. 1913. Situated between Alcester Lanes End and the Maypole, crowds thronged the area on summer weekends. Boats and punts could be hired and day trippers could buy tea at the wooden bungalows and huts and sit at the tables provided outside. A cup of tea during those summer week-end excursions was fundamental to their enjoyment. There was also an open stage where pierrots would perform to keep the crowds amused.

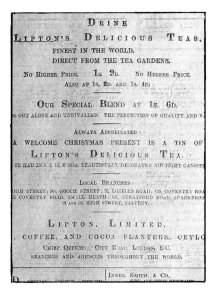

Thomas Lipton of Stobbs Cross had first become involved with tea in 1888. This Lipton's advertisement appeared on Christmas Eve, 1903, in the 'Birmingham Daily Mail'. Although their head office was in the City Road, London, they had local branches at High Street, Gooch Street, Lovell's Road, Coventry Road, Stratford Road, Sparkbrook and High Street, Saltley. They were also tea, coffee and cocoa planters in Ceylon.

In 1936 Woolworths in the Bull Ring were advertising their afternoon teas and Saturday-night suppers.

Co. The Treasury Tea Company were located not far from the Bull Ring at 101 Moor Street and a little further out of town, near Five Way, Edgbaston, was W. Whitby & Co., 24 Wyndham Street. The last tea merchant listed in 1928 was John Wilson & Sons (Birmingham) Ltd; according to their address – Well Street & Stables & Garages, 140 New John Street – their interests were not restricted to tea.

By 1934 the total number of Birmingham tea merchants had increased by six; some earlier names had gone and twelve new companies had been added:

Abbey Tea Co.	41 Lichfield Rd. Aston
British India Ceylon Tea Co.	39 Carrs Lane
Henry Cooper Tea Merchants Ltd.	15 Park Avenue, Soho Hill
Co-operators Dividend Ltd.	153A Corporation Street
Crawfords Teas Ltd (WHO)	15 Aston Road North
Customers Direct Supply Co.	9 Bond Street
Davey & Son	38 John Bright Street
Hop Tea Co.	93 Bristol Street
Horniman WH & FJ & Co. Ltd.	Liverpool Street
Ideal Tea Co.	52 Horse Shoe Lane, Sheldon
Imperial Supply Co.	180 Warstone Lane
Scott & Son	Suffolk House, Suffolk Street

When living on the Isle of Wight in about 1826 it was John Horniman who, with the help of a relative, Job Smith, started selling his packets of Horniman's Tea in foil-lined wrapping paper of a set weight. Until then almost all tea had been sold loose. His innovation set a pattern for all others to follow.

In 1899 Hornimans became incorporated and John's two sons, William Henry and Frederick John, added their initials to the company name. They were taken over by Lyons & Co., hence their Liverpool Street address in 1934 being that also of J. Lyons & Co.

At first Birmingham enjoyed a period of prosperity between the wars but then was caught up in the economic depression which affected the whole nation. It was during the 1930s that the depression had its full impact but, despite this, people still found comfort in their 'cuppa'.

In the 150 years since Widow Aston had opened the Birmingham Coffee House in 1774 the number of establishments serving tea had grown so that the people of Birmingham could take tea at numerous public places including tea gardens, tea rooms, hotels, railway stations, theatres, cinemas, tea dances, restaurants, cafeterias, even at some public parks and swimming baths. Factories and offices had their tea-breaks and men working outside would take their billycans for a brew-up on their coke-fired

In 1936 St James's restaurant in New Street was serving theatre teas and suppers.

Established in 1791 with a shop in New Street, Pattison & Co. Ltd expanded steadily so that by the 1950s they owned 31 tea shops, restaurants and cake shops in the Midlands.

braziers next to the holes they might be digging.

The first air raid siren sounded in Birmingham on the night of 25 June 1940 but it was not until the early morning of 9 August 1940 that the first bomb fell on the city, killing one man and injuring several others. This was the start of the air raids that were to bring death to many Birmingham people and destruction to their property. The British faced the trials and tribulations of war, with its air raids, rationing and deprivation, with a praiseworthy spirit and fortitude exemplified by the people of Birmingham.

TY·PHOO

4. A Business Built on a Leaf Edge

IN 1820 the old family grocery and druggists shop of Pratchett & Noble, which stood at the top of the Bull Ring, changed hands. The new owner was a young man of 24, William Sumner.

William Sumner settled in at once to running his new business and in 1820, having established himself, married into the family

97 and 98 Bull Ring in 1812. The grocery and druggist firm of Pratchett & Noble was established in the mid-eighteenth century. Richard Pratchett, the owner, had served for many years as one of Birmingham's Street Commissioners and was, in 1820, the High Bailiff for the city. In that year, however, being in poor health, he put his business up for sale.

of William Hutton, Birmingham's most famous historian. Two sons were born to them: John, in 1824, and William not long after. It was through John that the company was to flourish.

By 1830 William felt in a position to expand his business. An opportunity arose at Coleshill where he had close connections through his mother's family, the Lees; in 1830 he purchased a shop in Coleshill High Street. Pigot & Co.'s *National Commercial Directory* for 1835 for Coleshill lists him under the heading of 'Grocers & Tea Dealers' as

SUMNER, William (and Chymist and Druggist) Coleshill

In 1835 William also took on a Mr Portal as partner; their trade was stated to be druggists, tea dealers and oilmen. The tea they would have sold was from China, none other being then available. By 1845 the partnership with Mr Portal seems to have been dissolved; the *Post Office Directory of Birmingham, Warwick-*

Mr Portal became William Sumner's partner in 1835. The partnership lasted less than ten years; no mention is found of Mr Portal in either the 1845 'Post Office Directory' or in the 1847 Wrightson's 'Directory'.

shire and Part of Staffordshire for that year makes no mention of him in Coleshill but lists

SUMNER Wm. Druggist, grocer & tallow chandler
High Street & at Birmingham

The reason for Mr Portal's departure is not known. Perhaps it had something to do with William's desire to bring in his own son John to learn the trade. John Sumner was 21 years old at this juncture and probably already gaining experience in his father's shop; Mr Portal's departure would have given him the opportunity to take over the management at Coleshill for a time until he could join his father at 97 High Street, Birmingham.

Wright's *History, Gazeteer and Directory of Warwickshire* for 1850 is the first to announce John Sumner joining the business:

SUMNER Wm. & Son. Grocers & Tea Dealers, High Street, Coleshill

It was another two years before he became a part of the Birmingham concern. The listing in Slater's *Directory of Birmingham, 1852* describes William Sumner & Son as tea and coffee dealers although it was to be over fifty years before Sumner's multi-faceted business would concentrate solely on tea.

William Sumner at the age of 65. In 1852 he had moved house to Bennett's Hill in Washwood Heath but, two years later, at the age of 58, had decided to release the reins in favour of his two sons, John and William.

Two years later William gave the business to his two sons, John and William. We have no facts as to the latter's previous career but it is hardly likely that he would have been brought in to share the business without any training; it must be assumed that – like John – he had gained his experience at Coleshill, probably on the pharmaceutical side. The brothers' association lasted until 1863. They decided to go their separate ways, with William taking the Chemist & Druggists at 97 High Street, which had been his father's old shop, while John took the Grocers and Tea Dealers next door, 98 High Street which they had purchased in 1856 when it became vacant, together with the Coleshill shop.

If we are not happy at home, we cannot be happy elsewhere. It is the best proof of the virtues of a family circle to s... a happy ... ..

J. & W. SUMNER'S
HOUSEHOLD ALMANACK
AND
YEAR-BOOK OF USEFUL KNOWLEDGE
FOR
1860,
BEING BISSEXTILE OR LEAP YEAR;

CONTAINS

THE RISING AND SETTING OF THE SUN AND MOON;

A COPIOUS CALENDAR; LAW AND UNIVERSITY TERMS; ECLIPSES; TABLES OF STAMPS AND TAXES, &c.

A CHAPTER FOR PARENTS;

A WORD FOR THE BACHELORS;

Actibity not always Energy;

THE IMPORTANCE OF LITTLE THINGS;

ALSO,

GOLDEN MAXIMS. FOR THE HOUSEHOLD;

GOOD ADVICE IN SMALL COMPASS; CONTENT AND DISCONTENT; A WORD TO MOTHERS; HINTS BY A HOUSEWIFE; THE SECRET OF SUCCESS;

AND OTHER VALUABLE AND IMPORTANT MATTER.

PRESENTED ANNUALLY.

BIRMINGHAM:

PRINTED FOR J. & W. SUMNER, FAMILY GROCERS, &c.;
97 & 98, HIGH STREET, AND AT COLESHILL.

John and William issued their Almanack annually. Only this front cover and one inside page of the 1860 publication survive, together with a few pages of later issues.

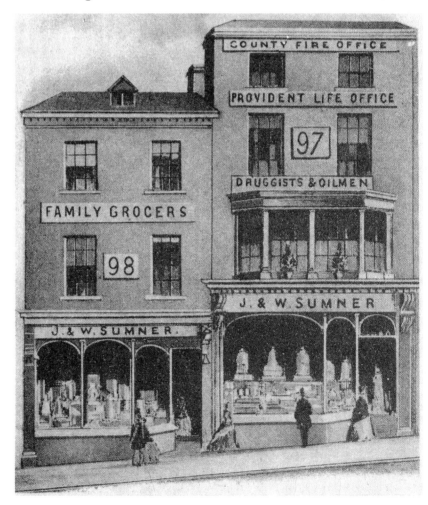

TEA   TEA
SIX POUNDS
of Great Strength and
Richness in Solid Japanned
Canister
18s.
JOHN SUMNER,
TEA AND ITALIAN
WAREHOUSE,
96, HIGH STREET,
BIRMINGHAM.

The Birmingham Daily Post,
April 1871.

John Sumner was keen to publicise his business; in April 1871 we find him advertising tea in the *Birmingham Daily Post*, the product in which he particularly seems to have taken more than a passing interest.

He also took out advertisements in Coleshill and Sutton Coldfield. In the *Sutton Coldfield and Erdington News*, Saturday, 28 January 1871, he inserted the following:

FOR CHRISTMAS PARTIES AND PRESENTS

We have a large, varied and carefully selected stock of desserts and fancy fruits.

Buns, bars, cossagues and other requests for the dessert table and ballroom.

John Sumner Tea & Italian Warehouse
98 High Street
Birmingham and at Coleshill

In 1854, William Sumner stepped down, and the signs over the Birmingham & Coleshill shops were altered to 'J. & W. Sumner'.
In 1856, the year that John's son, John, was born, the Sumner brothers acquired the next door premises of 98 High Street, previously occupied by J. Partridge.

Although he was no longer in partnership with his brother, John continued to produce the Almanack annually in his own name, being aware of its promotional value. On the cover of the 1875 publication he describes himself as 'John Sumner, Tea and Italian warehouse, Coffee Roaster and Wine Merchant'.

While John Sumner was busily pursuing his business interests certain events were taking place on the other side of the world that were to have a profound effect upon the future of the Sumner's grocery business. Around 1869 the coffee-rust disease

JOHN AND WILLIAM SUMNER, FAMILY GROCERS,

DRUGGISTS, OILMEN, &c.,

97 & 98, HIGH STREET, BIRMINGHAM,

AND AT

COLESHILL.

TEAS, COFFEES, AND COCOAS

Of the best Importations and Manufacture,

FOREIGN FRUITS & SPICES,

CROSSE & BLACKWELL'S PICKLES, MARMALADES, JELLIES, &c.

ANCHOVIES, CAPERS, FISH SAUCES, OLIVE OIL,

Wax and Spermaceti Lights, Wax Carriage Ditto, Wax Tapers, various sizes and colours; Wax and other Matches; Night Lights.

DIP & MOULD CANDLES, (own make) of BEST MATERIALS ONLY. KENSINGTON DITTO.

Price's Composition & Palmer's Metallic Candles.

COLEA OIL, CAMPHINE, PARAFFIN, AND PETROLINE.

Brown, Mottled, Yellow, and White Soap; Honey, Windsor, Olive Oil, ditto, &c.,

MANDY'S, WARD'S, AND TWELVETREES' WASHING POWDERS. AND CRYSTALS.

ARROW-ROOT, DESSERT; MIXED AND FANCY BISCUITS, &c.

Cardion and Patna Rice— Ground and Flour, Pearl Sago, Pearl Barley, Tapioca, Millet, Semolina, Arrow-root, Macaroni, Vermicelli, &c.

PATENT CORN FLOUR, ISINGLASS, GELATINE, EXTRACT OF CALVES' FEET.

KENT, WORCESTER, & SUSSEX HOPS.

PURE VINEGAR, SODA WATER, &c., &c.

Every other article in connection with either trades.

The surviving page from the 1860 Almanack gives an idea of J. & W. Sumner's wide-ranging stock.

(*Hemeleia vastatrix*) had appeared in Ceylon (now Sri Lanka) and had swept away the island's main cash crop and with it their coffee industry. Unable to stop the disease spreading they looked for a substitute to coffee. They discovered that tea would thrive and, by 1875, this new crop was sufficiently established for Ceylon to start exporting small quantities to England. It was tea from Ceylon in the early 1900s that was to become so important to the Sumners'.

The cover of John Sumner's 1875 Almanack. As a wine merchant, he had set up an extensive bottling operation across the road in the Old Court Yard – where Birmingham's first tea warehouse, Mansell's, had once been located.

98, High Street, Birmingham,
December, 1879.

Amid the intense competition, which a long period of depressed trade has called forth, I have gratefully (and with pleasure) to acknowledge the good share of business which, notwithstanding, has fallen to my lot; and the confidence that has been accorded to me for so many years.

It is, and always has been, my earnest endeavour and study to meet the wishes of my Customers—to promote in every way the feeling of trustfulness which should exist between buyer and seller; always my desire to right anything wrong, or amend anything amiss; to exchange or return money for any article which for reasons may either not be required or liked.

To those who may see benefits in a novel method of conducting business, I merely ask, in all fairness, to be placed on the same footing,—that is absolutely necessary. To secure advantages, Goods must be paid for on or before delivery; or to save trouble, Money may be deposited, and drawn against in Goods. This system has its drawbacks and annoyances—as loss of interest, &c., &c. Nor can it be expected that in the staple commodities of the trade, which form the heavier and principal items of expenditure in a family, amateur shopkeepers can compete with those who to their continued study of and access to, the Best Markets—from which their rivals are excluded—have added the experience which years of unremitting attention can alone supply.

My Customers may be assured of best value for money, and attention at all times.

I am, respectfully,

Geo Sumner

```
┌─────────────────────────────────────────────────────────┐
│                   THIS  LIST                            │
│  When ordering goods will be useful as a remembrancer.  In all cases │
│  please state definitely what is required and if in any particular sized │
│                      packages, &c.                       │
│  ─────────────────────────────────────────────────────  │
│     We shall feel at all times pleased by a visit from our Customers; there are │
│  frequent Novelties and Additions to Stock, which may not be thought of during │
│  the hurry of our travellers' periodical calls upon them. │
│  ─────────────────────────────────────────────────────  │
│  TEAS.—Black—Green—Mixed.  See pages 4 and 5.           │
│  COFFEE—Berries—Ground—Mixed with Chicory.  See page 6. │
│  COCOA AND CHOCOLATE—Fry's, Epp's, Cadbury's, Menier's, and Taylor's. │
│     The manufactures of these and other eminent makers we have in great │
│     variety.  Sumner's Homoeopathic Chocolate is an excellent preparation. │
│  SUGARS—Raw (old-fashioned West India), the produce of Demerara, Jamaica, │
│     Barbadoes, &c.; Moist, (White British-made); Refined (Loaf), Castor Sugar, │
│     Sugar Candy, Icing Sugar, Brewing Sugar, &c.  For Wine, Marmalade, and │
│     Preserves, ask particularly for Cane-made Sugar. │
│  SPICES—Pepper—White, Black, Cayenne, and Jamaica.  Nutmegs, Mace, │
│     Cloves, Cinnamon, Ginger, and an excellent Mixture for Pickling.  We │
│     grind these on our own premises, and can guarantee Purity and Quality. │
│  MUSTARD—Various qualities by Keen, Robinson and Co.; Sadler, Firth and │
│     Ross, &c. │
│  FARINACEOUS ARTICLES—Rice, Sago, Tapioca, Arrowroot, Corn Flour, │
│     Oswego, Semolina, Manaccasup, Maizena, Scotch and Fine Oatmeal, &c., &c. │
│  DRIED FRUITS—Raisins, Valencia, Sultana, Currants, Candied Peel, Prunes, │
│     Normandy Pippins, &c. │
│  DESSERT FRUITS—Muscatel Raisins, Almonds, Figs, Dates, French Plums, │
│     Preserved Ginger, Crystalized Apricots, Peaches, &c., &c. │
│  BISCUITS—Huntley and Palmer's; Carr and Co.'s; Mackenzie and Mackenzie's. │
│     Our large and quick sale enables us to supply these constantly fresh.  Also │
│     Cakes by the same Makers.  See page 7 │
│  PICKLES, SAUCES, FRENCH AND ITALIAN GOODS—Our assort- │
│     ment is very large and varied.  We have always the best of the novelties early │
│     to hand. │
│  JAMS, JELLIES, MARMALADE—From the best manufacturers. │
│  SALAD OIL—The finest we can obtain in flasks, bottles, &c., and for frying fish. │
│  WINES.—I respectfully solicit trial of Sample Bottles, feeling assured │
│     of their giving satisfaction.  See pp. 8, 9, 10, and 20, 22. │
│  VINEGARS—Pure Malt and Distilled—these guaranteed by the analyses of Drs. │
│     Ure and Herapath.  See p. 12.  French, Shallot, Tarragon, &c., &c. │
│  SOAPS—Household, Mottled, Yellow, White and Scouring.  Dry Soap, Borax, │
│     Cold Water Soap.  Toilet Soap in great variety, from the best makers. │
│  CANDLES—Wax, Spermaceti, Paraffin (many kinds of these), Composites, Car- │
│     riage Candles, Lamp Candles, Piano Candles, Wax Tapers, Night Lights, │
│     Reflectors, Candle Ornaments, Wax Wick for lighting, &c.  Best quality Dips. │
│  SUNDRIES—Bird Seeds, Blacking (liquid and paste), Black Lead, Cream │
│     Tartar, Carbonate of Soda, Italian Juice, Baking Powder, Bay Salt, Saltpetre, │
│     Beeswax, Furniture Cream, Safety Matches, and Wax Vestas, Colza Oil, │
│     Paraffin Oil, pure and safe, Benzoline, &c. │
│  ─────────────────────────────────────────────────────  │
│  Any Article not in Stock we shall be happy to obtain on short notice. │
│                                                          │
│        FOR LIST OF JOURNEYS SEE PAGES 2 & 3.            │
│  ─────────────────────────────────────────────────────  │
│     Families desirous of being waited upon will please apply or write to │
│  98, High Street, Birmingham, or Coleshill.            │
└─────────────────────────────────────────────────────────┘
```

John Sumner's 1879 Almanack shows his businesslike attitude as well as his comprehensive stock — including 'Sumner's homoeopathic chocolate' — at Birmingham and Coleshill. Throughout 1878 John Sumner ran regular advertisements on the front page of 'The Coleshill Chronicle'. From grocer to veterinary chemist, he is shown to be a man of many parts.

According to Kelly's 1880 'Directory of Warwickshire', his home was in Blythe Road, Coleshill, from where he would travel each day to 98 High Street, Birmingham.

Until the year 1888 there had been no indication as to what John Sumner's son John had been doing with his life. We do know, however, that he was born on 26 February 1856 in Birmingham and had been educated privately; also that he had a younger brother, Sidney Herbert Sutton who was born in 1867 and died at the comparatively early age of 32 in 1899. There was also a sister, whose married name would be Mary Augusta

JOHN SUMNER,

TEA

Is now an article of such large and general consumption that, to obtain it Good and Cheap, to combine Excellence with Economy is naturally an object of solicitude with all Purchasers. This important subject has been our study for many years. The opportunities we possess of buying in the best Markets The Teas of India and China, the Great Variety and Number of Samples we have offered for selection, from the largest Importers in the World, enable us to offer these on exceptionally favourable terms.

The present Duty on Tea is Sixpence, and ¼ per cent. per lb. When it is, as so often untruthfully and unblushingly asserted that no Tea better than 2s. or 2s. 6d. per lb. can be obtained—test the veracity by your own judgment on comparison.

		s.	d.
Strong and nice flavoured Tea—good whole leaf ...... per lb.		2	0
The Combined Qualities of Freshness, Strength, and Briskness have insured this a most favourable reception at the hands of the Public, as the large quantity now selling indicates	,,	2	6
"The Standard." This Peculiar and Favourite Combination was under the old Duty 3s. 8d. per lb., and since the reduction 3s. 2d., is now 3s. The characteristics that have made it popular for so many years have been strictly maintained; it is a Rich, Rough, Pekoe Souchong, Flavoured Tea of High Quality	...,,	3	0a
"An Indian Tea," same price as the last. This has Distinguishing Good Qualities, entirely diverse from the others, and is deservedly much esteemed	,,	3	0b
Finest Lapsang Souchong—Finest Kaisow—Finest Moning Congous. Each of these has a distinct character; they are Mellow, Rich, Ripe, Old-Fashioned Teas. To Connoisseurs and those who state Tea is not so good as it used to be. Let them try samples of these	,,	3	6
"Drawing Room Tea." This is a combination in proper proportions of The Finest Teas that India and China produce—a Tea for occasions, a Drawing Room Tea of the Highest Class. Nothing Finer or Choicer is obtainable	,,	•4	0

We supply the above in parcels, in strong useful Family Canisters containing six pounds, in lead lined Caddy Boxes, from fifteen to twenty pounds; in Half Chests about sixty, and Chests about one hundred pounds. On these three last the overweights allowed are respectively half-pound, pound, and two pounds, in itself a good discount. Carriage will be prepaid, and a discount of twopence per pound allowed for Cash on all parcels of six pounds and upwards.

Hotel Keepers, Schoolmasters and Mistresses will find advantages unsurpassed in the trade.

98, High Street, Birmingham

During his time in the grocery trade, John had become something of a specialist in tea. This he demonstrated in 1863 by publishing a popular treatise on 'Tea: Historical, Botanical, Chemical'. These pages from his 1879 Almanack show both his expertise and his wide stock of China and Indian teas.

Sumner-Kneale and who would play a most vital rôle in the story of the formation of Sumner's 'Ty-Phoo' Tea Ltd.

Nothing had been mentioned about John junior having previously been involved in his father's business, but it may be that like his father he had worked at both Coleshill and Birmingham gaining experience after finishing his education. It was not until

Tea Merchant,

GREEN TEAS.

		s.	d.
Gunpowder, good .... per lb.		3	0
Gunpowder, fine and good .... ,,		3	6
Gunpowder, very fine Moyune Tea	,,	4	0
Ditto strong burnt rich fragrant Tea..............	,,	4	6
Ditto finest Moyune, curiously strong fine Tea...	,,	5	0
Young Hyson, good liquor and clean.................2s.	,,	2	6
Ditto finer	,,	3	0
Ditto very fine and choice .... 3s. 6d.	,,	4	6
Ouchain, fine to finest .... 4s.	,,	5	0
Hyson, fine old fashioned Tea .... 4s.	,,	4	6

We can assure our Customers that sound fine pure Green Tea is by no means deleterious. Like many other good things when used in moderation it may not only be enjoyed with impunity but taken with benefit. We strongly recommend a slight admixture of Green with Black Tea.

ASSAM, OOLONG, AND SCENTED TEAS.

		s.	d.
Good Canton Orange Pekoe ... . 2s. 6d. per lb.		3	0
Fine ditto ditto ditto	,,	3	6
Extra fine ditto ditto ditto	,,	4	0

These Teas are very peculiar, the leaf is long, black, wiry, and altogether unique in appearance.

| Very choice Foo Chow Orange Pekoe .... 3s. 6d. | ,, | 4 | 0 |

This is a jessamine-scented Tea. It is quite a different class, both in appearance and flavour. from the Cantons. The leaf is small, amber-coloured, with golden-flowered tips. It is much used, and when blended with other Teas gives a particularly fine and delicate flavour.

Good Caper ....2s. 6d.	,,	3	0
Fine ditto	,,.	3	6
Extra fine ditto, Curious	,,	4	0

These Teas are rough and pungent, and when blended with other Teas, have the same effect as Green Tea, at the same time imparting a very fragrant and delicate flavour.

and Coleshill.

he was 31 years of age that he was officially brought into the business. The first to record the fact was Kelly's *Directory of Birmingham* of 1888 where it lists:

SUMNER, John & Son – 98 High Street, Birmingham

When father and son had been in partnership for four years a

The Coleshill Chronicle

Business Addresses.

TEA WAREHOUSE & DISPENSARY,

COLESHILL.

THE ALTERATIONS we have recently made have enabled us to devote the premises added entirely to the DRUG and DISPENSING DEPARTMENT, under the care of the manager, and a qualified assistant. We are now enable to pay the greatest attention to all PHYSICIANS' PRESCRIPTIONS and FAMILY RECEIPTS that may be entrusted to us, and to assure our customers that none but the Purest Chemical Drugs that can be obtained will be used in their preparation.

GENUINE PATENT MEDICINES. All kinds of MEDICAL APPLIANCES either in stock or obtained at the shortest notice. HORSE and CATTLE MEDICINES.

JNO. SUMNER,

COLESHILL AND BIRMINGHAM.

CHRISTMAS!

FRUITS OF MANY COUNTRIES
Dried, Preserved, and Crystallised.

CHAMPAGNES, CLARET, SHERRY, PORT, &c.,
Of very choice qualities. Trial of samples solicited.

CAKES, BISCUITS, CRACKERS, &c.
In great variety.

JOHN SUMNER,
TEA, WINE, AND ITALIAN WAREHOUSE, COLESHILL AND BIRMINGHAM.

These advertisements in the 'Coleshill Chronicle' in 1878 show the diversity of products and services John Sumner had to offer. He advertised regularly in the 'Chronicle' which carried his message to his customers in and around the small country town of Coleshill.

JOHN SUMNER

Wishes to call attention to the following Superior Preparations:—

SUMNER'S ALTERATIVE CONDITION POWDER FOR HORSES.

This preparation is unequalled for excellence, and specially recommended as an alterative and Tonic medicine, which not only gives to the coat a beautiful gloss and texture, but by Strengthening the Digestion and Purifying the Blood, gives to the animal that health and vigour which tends to increase so much the value of any Horse, either for sale or work.—In tins containing 1 pound each.

SUMNER'S COUGH BALLS : AN EFFECTUAL REMEDY.

SUMNER'S DIURETIC OR URINE BALLS.

SUMNER'S PURGING BALLS.

SUMNER'S CORDIAL BALLS: For horses in low condition, or after a hard day's hunting, &c.

SUMNER'S OINTMENT FOR GREASE IN HORSES, AND FOR CRACKED HEELS.

SUMNER'S WHITE OILS.

If used at once, in accordance with the directions printed on each bottle, is an almost unfailing remedy for Sprains, Bruises, Kicks (when the skin is not broken), and for weakness of the muscles.

————

These are from old and well-tried Recipes ; can always be used with the greatest safety.

————

JOHN SUMNER, CHEMIST, COLESHILL.

FLIES AND MAGGOTS'

————

TO FARMERS AND SHEEP OWNERS.

————

SUMNER'S
CELEBRATED FLY POWDER

Is the best known preventative of Maggots in Sheep and Lambs. Its NAUSEOUS FLAVOUR AND PUNGENT SMELL render it impossible for Flies to attack any sheep dusted over with this Powder. Sold in tins with perforated tops at 1s. each or 11s. 6d. per dozen. Each tin will dress 14 Sheep, or 20 Lambs. Full directions on the label. Prepared only by

JOHN SUMNER,

VETERINARY CHEMIST, COLESHILL, AND AT 98, HIGH STREET, BIRMINGHAM.

N.B.—The Fly Powder is prepared in two colors, grey and brown.

decision was made to sell off the shop in Coleshill, which William Sumner had purchased in 1830, and concentrate their efforts in Birmingham. The last record for the Coleshill shop appears in Kelly's *Directory of Warwickshire* for 1892 which reads:

SUMNER & Son Pharmaceutical Chemists, Grocers & Wine Merchants. High Street, Coleshill.

A serious disruption to business occurred in 1894. In an announcement to their customers in the *Birmingham Daily Post* dated 15 June 1894, they explained that they had received short notice to quit 98 High Street, Bull Ring, as the premises were required for a new railway tunnel to be built.

For a short period they operated from number 10 High Street, which must have been most unsatisfactory because they were

---

JOHN SUMNER

Is now a holder of some remarkable fine Kent, Sussex, Worcester, German, and Belgian

H O P S

Which he has every confidence in offering as being, both in strength and quality, excellently suited for Spring Brewing, and will be glad to hand samples to consumers.

FINE BREWING SUGAR.

———

THE TEA, WINE, AND HOP WAREHOUSE, COLESHILL & BIRMINGHAM.

AUTUMN WHEAT SOWING SEASON, 1878.

———

BLUE VITRIOL (PURE SULPHATE OF COPPER),
Specially recommended. POWDERED and in the LUMP, and packed in any size parcels required

———

SUMNER'S ALTERATIVE CONDITION BALLS
FOR HORSES,
HORSE BALLS, BLISTERS, &c.

———

PREPARED ONLY BY

J O H N   S U M N E R ,

VETERINARY AND AGRICULTURAL CHEMIST, COLESHILL
AND AT 98, HIGH STREET, BIRMINGHAM.

---

having to share it with the Home and Colonial Stores Ltd. However it was not long before more suitable premises became available further up the hill. This was Hutton House, 25 & 26 High Street, which had been built in 1775 by John Sumner senior's kinsman, William Hutton, the Birmingham historian. Hutton House proved to be extremely suitable and convenient, being in a very prominent position in the town and only a short distance from their large block of warehouses and bottling stores in the Old Court Yard.

From 1895 onwards the Sumners' old premises at 97 & 98 High Street would not appear in any Birmingham directory. But over the previous 80 years they had provided the family with a fine location on which they could build a steady trade and acquire a reasonable standard of living. A new century was

Whilst John pressed on with his business, brother William was to sell his off and in 1883 No. 97 High Street was occupied by Partridge & Co., Ironmongers.

John Sumner was 64 years old when he brought his son John into partnership in 1888.

The Coleshill shop photographed during the Silver Jubilee celebrations of Coleshill's vicar, John Pinney.

John Sumner at the age of eighty.

This postcard taken from 1901–1905 looks down New Street from the corner of Corporation Street. Hutton House is at the far end in the centre and has 'SUMNERS' in large letters on top.

dawning, bringing with it a dramatic change to the Sumners' business.

The year 1900 began with John Sumner senior coming up to his 75th birthday and son John approaching his 44th. Business was good, they had extensive wine and spirit stock and plant, a stout and cider bottling branch and their grocery side, apart from considerable stock, employed twenty horses and vans and six travellers.

Their bank manager had been associated with the Sumners since the 1870s and was accommodating enough to allow them a generous overdraft, being confident that the business was sound and well run.

Two large windows of the shop overlooked High Street and displayed a wide range of goods. Inside were a number of assistants standing at a long counter behind which were well-stocked shelves. Some display cabinets and scales stood on the counter and a few chairs were strategically placed around the shop for customers' convenience. Illumination for the interior and the windows was provided by gas and incandescent mantle. The streets outside were also illuminated by gas light. Gas had first become available in Birmingham in 1817 with the formation of the Birmingham Gaslight Co.

47

John Sumner junior was interested in the town in which he earned a living. He had read Hutton's *History of Birmingham* (1781) with interest, but when he moved into Hutton House he had a direct link with the illustrious ancestor who had been responsible for erecting the building. He was particularly drawn to a passage in Hutton's book relating to some of the material used in its construction:

In 1775 I took down an old house of wood and plaster which had stood for 208 years having been erected in 1567, thirty-one years after the dissolution of the Abbeys. The foundations of this old house seem to have been built with stones from the Priory; perhaps more than twenty loads. These appeared in a variety of forms and sizes, highly finished in the Gothic taste, parts of porticos, windows, ceilings etc. some fluted, some cyphered and otherwise ornamented, yet complete as in the first day they were

Before the Sumners had taken it over, Hutton House had been occupied by the Badman Bros, tobacconists, and by Mme Marion Simons' mantle warehouse.

left by the chisel. The greatest part of them were destroyed by the workmen; some others I used again in the fireplace of an under kitchen. Perhaps they are the only perfect fragments that remain of that venerable edifice, which once stood the monument of ancient piety, the ornament of the town and the envy of the priest out of place.

Having read this, John junior went into the kitchen of Hutton House and discovered the remains of the priory to which Hutton referred. Such was his desire to preserve for the town the only

The 'Priory' Stone now on display in Birmingham Museum was rescued by John Sumner Jnr from the kitchen of Hutton House. He mounted it on a piece of oak with a suitable inscription and presented it to the museum it being the only known remains of that venerable edifice The Old Priory.

The 'Priory' Stone – Reproduced by permission of Birmingham Museum and Art Gallery.

known surviving remains that he had a carved piece of stone
mounted on a section of oak with a suitable inscription added,
which he then presented to the Birmingham Museum where it
can be viewed in the local history section.

A very early Typhoo advertisement.

John Sumner senior, now advanced in years, left the running
of the shop to his son. In spite of having a successful wine, spirit
and grocery business, John junior had long sought a speciality
he could develop outside his retail business but so far nothing
had presented itself that might be worth pursuing.

His chance came in 1903 as a result of his sister, Mary
Augusta, suffering from indigestion. She had long endured the
complaint when somebody had sent her a packet of very special
tea with a promise of a cure. The tea itself was in tiny particles
and, as tea in those days was of the large leaf variety, she viewed
it with some suspicion. But since it was different from ordinary
tea which was known to aggravate her problem, she tried it and
to her delight found that it gave her great relief.

She wished to share her discovery with others and tried it out
on her gardener, a fellow sufferer, with like result. Spurred on,
she tried it out on some of her friends who were also troubled
with indigestion and they, too, benefited.

In her enthusiasm Mary Augusta approached her grocer
brother John. Having explained the benefits she and her friends
had obtained from drinking this special tea, she asked, 'Why

A 1917 half-pound packet.

don't you sell this tea?' Those few words spoken by Mary to her brother John were to be the catalyst to a great business which was to provide success to its founder and a means of livelihood for others up to the present day.

John junior gave serious thought to his sister's question and considered that tea possessed of such unusual qualities had possibilities. He then consulted a friend in the wholesale tea trade, who was most likely to have been J. H. Brindley, founder of the Priory Tea and Coffee Co., in Dale End, Birmingham.

When he told his friend of this tea and said, 'I believe there is a future in it: and I think of securing a break of 30 chests to try it out and spending £200 in advertising it', his friend replied, 'Don't do it. You will lose your money, certain. The public will never buy any tea so small as this. They'll call it dust.'

In spite of his friend's foreboding, he went ahead and secured the 30 chests. Rather than sell it loose over the counter, he decided to put it in a packet under a brand name. The criteria he placed upon choosing a name for his tea were:

1. The name must be distinctive and unlike others.
2. It must be one which would trip off the tongue.
3. It must be one which could be protected by registration.

He spent many sleepless nights trying to think of a good name. Many were thought of and discarded until finally he decided upon the name 'Typhoo' Tipps. It had an Oriental sound, was alliterative with tea and, most important, Somerset House had no objection to the name 'Typhoo'. The word 'Tipps' could not be registered, although it appeared on the packets for some years and was copied by many imitators even to the eccentric 'pp' which originated in a printer's error.

The first cardboard packets with the name 'Typhoo' Tipps Tea printed on them were filled by girls using scoops, then weighed on the scales, glued and sealed. R. H. Burton, who had started working for the Sumners in 1884 and was in at the birth of 'Typhoo' tea, noted that written in pencil upon one side of the first 'Typhoo' bin were the words, 'Packed this week 577 lbs. November 1903'.

Having been packed, the tea now had to be sold. The shop was still retail and as an inducement to their customers a generous jar of cream was offered to each purchaser of a pound of 'Typhoo' tea. It was not long before most of their customers had been converted to drinking 'Typhoo' tea.

When recalling those early days R. H. Burton wrote, many years later:

CORPORATION STREET,
BIRMINGHAM.

I remember quite well how in 1903 he (John Sumner junior) first introduced the new tea; how everyone concerned was worked up to enthusiasm about it, the assistants pushing it at the counter, and the travellers on their rounds; how one scheme after another was tried to gain the notice of the general public. There was no machinery then, only the old hand scales and scoop upon an extemporised counter, and packed at speed of not a packet a minute.

Built in 1878, Corporation Street was lined with shops on both sides. John Sumner rented a shop in Corporation Street and had a row of girls packing 'Typhoo' in the large window. Passers-by were able to pop in and enjoy a quick cup of 'Typhoo'.

So in November 1903 'Typhoo' tea was born at Hutton House, High Street, Birmingham, the site of which is presently occupied by a bookshop. The new tea quickly caught on. Once people bought it they seldom changed to any other and although it was slightly more expensive, it would also go further and so proved more economical in the end. In addition, its beneficial digestive qualities had great appeal.

Satisfied customers provided ample recommendation and the fame of 'Typhoo' soon spread beyond the shop's regular clientele. Customers of other traders began calling in for it at the counter. One day a grocer called in and asked if he could buy 'Typhoo' tea on wholesale terms, as some of his customers insisted upon having it. John Sumner was only too happy to oblige. So he began his wholesale agency trade.

John Sumner junior, c. 1904.

Soon others followed, and so a traveller was employed to call on shops. Demand grew fast and John did his utmost to promote his new tea. He took a shop in Corporation Street where a row of girls in the window packed the tea while inside cups of tea with cream and biscuits were served.

This was followed by John taking a stand at a trade exhibition at Bingley Hall, Birmingham, where two long rows of girls packed 'Typhoo' tea and, in a buffet alongside, cups of tea were sold. It proved a great attraction and created much interest resulting in many new agencies, both in Birmingham and outside towns.

In spite of competition from over sixty tea merchants in Birmingham, including such names as Barrow's, Priory Tea, Ridgway's, Lipton's and Neale's Tea Stores, the new 'Typhoo' tea had been launched and was doing well. Sales increased throughout 1904 and its growth was most encouraging. As the business increased, so more capital was needed. There was none available from the old established grocery business for much of its money was locked up in its big stocks, heavy book debts, twenty horses and vans. The only alternative was to approach the bank.

Just at this time the Sumners' old bank manager retired. He had known the firm for over thirty years and had watched the new development with interest and approval. He was replaced by a younger man who, when approached for financial assistance, took an opposite and uncompromising stance and called for the existing overdraft to be paid off in no uncertain terms.

A serious crisis now existed and, as John Sumner later recalled: 'The situation became electric.' Not only was no further finance available, but also he was now faced with the task of paying off his overdraft.

He had to come to a decision quickly. Should he throw away the new tea business into which he had put so much time and effort and which was now on the brink of success? Having anxiously considered the situation he decided to burn his boats, sell the grocery business which had been his father's and grandfather's, back his intuition and trust the future to 'Typhoo'.

The year was now 1905. John Sumner had hoped to find a buyer quickly but, as the months passed, no suitable buyer presented himself. All this time the bank became more pressing for repayment of the overdraft. It would seem the business was too large for a private purchaser but of not sufficient importance to float as a public company.

He decided that if he could not sell the business, he would scrap it, forego the goodwill, realise the stock, book debts and fixtures and close the shop. After paying off the overdraft he would stake his all on 'Typhoo'. Fortunately the lease of Hutton House was nearing its end and he could move to other premises to carry on producing his 'Typhoo' tea. He approached a leading local firm who, in consideration of the value of the established journeys of the business, bought the grocery stock and agreed to collect the debts. Another bought the wine and spirit stock and plant, also the ale, stout, and cider, bottling branch in the Old Court Yard.

Having disposed of his grocery business he now had sufficient funds to pay off the bank. This he did and promptly closed his account. The short-sighted attitude of that manager had lost his bank a major account; he would have a long time to regret his hasty behaviour.

Whilst causing John Sumner so much heart-searching and nearly wrecking the new company, that bank manager had, in fact, hastened its severence from the grocery business, and, in doing so, had unwittingly helped in the development of 'Typhoo'.

In the meantime, however, John Sumner junior had set up his new venture as a separate business and, backed with finance from a few friends, formed a little private company with £2,000 in shares and £800 debentures. On the 29th day of July, 1905 Sumner's 'Typhoo' Tea Ltd was incorporated, ready to face what the future might hold. The identity and holding of the first shareholders is worth recording:

Benjamin Richardson 4 Old Swan Lane, London Wholesale Druggist	400
Richard Sydney Potter Hawkeswell, Coleshill Farmer	150 preference
Richard Potter Hawkeswell, Coleshill, Retired Farmer	100 preference
James Henry Brindley 75 Hall Road, Handsworth, Birmingham, Director of a Public Company	25 preference
Frederick William Hart Carrs Lane, Birmingham Managing Director of a Public Company	125 preference
John Sumner junior The Cottage, Yardley, Birmingham Provision Merchant	50 ordinary
Martha Elizabeth Sumner The Cottage, Yardley, Birmingham Wife of John Sumner junior	200 preference

When John junior had embarked upon selling his new tea in November 1903 he had started off with 30 chests, but by 1905 the business had expanded and consequently required larger quantities of the small-leaf tea. The answer to how many chests were required at the commencement of Sumner's 'Typhoo' Tea Ltd was provided in 1964 by John's son J. R. Hugh Sumner: 'It was in 1905 my father started the company in quite a little way. He went to Ceylon and brought back 200 chests of tea, mainly fannings.'

John Sumner did not immediately move out of Hutton House but remained there during 1906 and for a while even took over the premises next door at number 24 which previously had been occupied by the 'Pitman's' Restaurant Refreshment Rooms. This is confirmed by an entry in Kelly's *Directory of Birmingham* for 1906:

24, 25 & 26 High Street. Sumner's 'Typhoo' Tea Ltd, tea mers.

At the end of 12 months' trading including, two months prior to incorporation, the trade account covering the period 31 May

J. H. Brindley was the founder of the Priory Tea & Coffee Company, Dale End, Birmingham, and a good friend of John Sumner Junior giving great support and assistance in the early years, subsequently becoming a director of Sumner's Typhoo Tea Ltd.

1905 to 31 May 1906 showed sales amounting to £13,631 10s 9½d and stock of tea £629 0s 9d. The wage bill was £589 5s 1d advertising £734 8s 4d, purchases of tea totalled £10,218 7s 8d. Trading profit for the two months 31 May to 29 July 1905 was £143 8s 7d and from 29 July 1905 to 31 May 1906 was £181 2s 7d. On the balance sheet, goodwill and trade marks were put at £460.

He had survived the first year and shown a small profit, he had also silenced his critics who said he could never sell the small-leafed tea, otherwise known as fannings. This tea customarily had been swept off the floor, burnt or dug in around the roots of tea plants in Ceylon. But John Sumner had established a market for it and demand continued to grow, which made other tea merchants sit up and take notice.

In promoting his tea John Sumner junior drew attention to it being from the edge of the leaf, devoid of the fibrous stalk which contained tannin – thus making it pure tea leaf and tannin-less. Not only could such pure leaf-edge tea produce eighty more cups to the pound than ordinary large leaf but the latter contained much stalk and tannin which, he pointed out, was

The entrance to Castle Street is just beyond the double awning on the right of this Edwardian view of the High Street.

injurious to the nerves and digestion. He had had first-hand experience of the benefits obtained from his tea by indigestion sufferers through his sister Mary Augusta who had first drawn attention to its therapeutic properties.

To back up his claims he enlisted the support of many doctors who recommended his tea as giving relief to, or even curing, acute dyspepsia. In addition to the doctors' support, his tea also found outlets through many chemists' shops.

By the end of 1906 he had moved out of Hutton House into Castle Street where he rented the top two floors. Today Castle Street, a very narrow street running down from the High Street alongside Marks and Spencer, has been blocked off.

In those early days the workforce was small. Besides John Sumner junior there was Richard Burton; the tea was packed by ten girls. Miss Lucas, the superintendent of the office, started in March 1907 and including herself there were only three girls in the office. A typewriting machine and Roneo duplicating machine were part of the office equipment and there was one telephone. There were also 1661 agents' stamps, which may have been used for addressing envelopes sent to them. Miss

57

E. E. Akers, head of sales, also joined in 1907. The other occupiers of the building were Gibbs, George & Co., Corsett Manufacturers and Bromley WR & Co, Provision Merchant. As time went by they moved out, allowing 'Typhoo' to take over the whole building.

On 31 December 1906 stock-taking took place and from these records we are able to obtain some interesting information. The advertising department list gives us an insight into the materials and methods used by John Sumner in his advertising and promotions, and from this list we show below some of the items:

2,300	Shelf Slips
2,400	Window Bills
250	Tannin Circulars
90	Packet Cards
125	Tannin less slips
160	Cards ('This Tea Relieves' etc.)
21	Tea Pot Show Stands
12,000	Drug Circulars
150	Doctors' Address Lists
35,000	R U Circulars
648	Fairy Bells
5	Small Restaurant Pots
24	Typhoo Patent Pots
5	Large Flowery Blue Pots
11	Medium Flowery Blue Pots
3	Small Flowery Blue Pots
2	Ponies (£28)
	Horses and Harness Utensils

As early as 1906 John Sumner was having his own special 'Typhoo' patent teapots made for sale to his customers. He took the opportunity of inserting circulars into the packets of tea relating to the effects of tannin contained in ordinary tea and others about his tannin-less tea. Picture cards – similar to cigarette cards – covering a whole range of subjects were also inserted and these became very collectable.

On 1 January 1907 tea stocks stood at 3,246 lbs of which 1,351 lbs were in ½ lb packets. There was a filling machine valued at £12 which may have been the one worked by a pedal to drop the tea into the packet, a tea hopper into which the tea was tipped to be fed down to the filling machine, and two platform weighing machines, one for 2 cwt, the other 1 cwt.

From its inception Sumner's 'Typhoo' Tea Ltd made steady progress and continued to grow. By the year 1909 John Sumner had the pleasure of having repaid all debts. His balance sheet was free from debentures; the preference shares, except for a few hundred retained by certain relatives, together with all the ordinary shares, were safely in his own hands. John Sumner, in

This photograph taken in the early 1900s shows some male members of the Sumner family.

John Sumner, founder of Typhoo, rests his arms on the back of the chair whilst his father sporting a white beard relaxes for the photographer.

later years, referred to the profit of £720 on the 1909 balance sheet which, 'made him a proud and happy man'.

He was not the only one who was charting his progress. In 1909 he was approached by a wholesale tea house with an offer of amalgamation and a seat on the board. After having gone through the trials of the past few years, why should he let someone else obtain the benefit of his hard work now that the business was on a sound financial footing and with tremendous possibilities? Preferring to retain his independence, he declined the offer.

Now that the company was financially out of trouble and he had limited funds at his disposal, John Sumner felt reasonably justified in taking a three months' trip to the East to study tea at the source of supply.

Leaving the business in the hands of his co-director and Mr R. Burton, the works manager, John Sumner set sail for Ceylon. Through the introductions he had taken out he was able to get in touch with the heart of the island's tea industry and managed to arrange a buying, blending agency which would effect great economies in the prime cost of his tea.

After formal discussions he appointed agents in Colombo to act for 'Typhoo' in buying, blending and shipping the special leaf-edge tea. This was to be acquired from the Ceylon auctions and tea estates, then blended, then shipped in 70-lb (31.75 kg) chests. The size of the chests was important for they were to be re-used in England to hold 50 lbs of packed stock for delivery to customers.

A most important factor in the agreement was that all blending was to be done in Ceylon, so all the shipped tea would be ready to be put into the packets on arrival. This eliminated the need for expensive blending equipment in Birmingham, saving space and keeping down costs. This, together with the improved purchasing facilities, enabled John Sumner to offer to the trade a better margin of profit, whilst reducing the price of 'Typhoo' to the public.

He returned to England satisfied that his newly appointed agents were men of integrity and that the agreement would work to the mutual benefit of both parties. As 'Typhoo' flourished, so the Ceylon agents would also reap profitable rewards. With a distance of 6,900 miles between them it was decided to keep the personal contact alive through yearly visits by either someone from 'Typhoo' to Ceylon or from Ceylon to Birmingham.

The following years were of satisfactory trading and steady growth. John Sumner had every reason to feel proud that his venture had taken off so well. He had regular supplies of his leaf-edge tea and a growing home market. He also had an

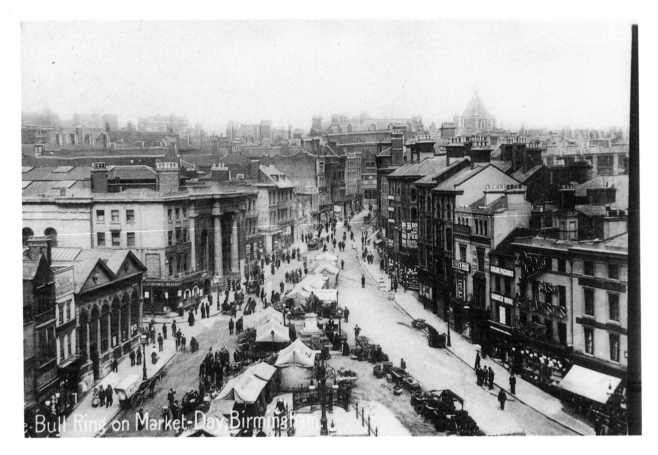

Bull Ring on Market-Day, Birmingham

Postmarked 21 July 1911, this postcard shows the Bull Ring on market day.

enthusiastic and loyal staff who were prepared to put up with the antiquated Castle Street premises because the firm was so small that they felt like a happy family.

John Sumner adopted a paternalistic attitude to the girls on his staff. One young girl who started at Castle Street in November 1911 when the company was only six years old was Clara Edith Simister – 'Sim' to the other girls. Born on 5 May 1897, she was 14 when, as she recently described, she was interviewed by Miss Lucas for an office job and taken on at 4 shillings (80p) per week. Later she was to learn Pitman's shorthand, eventually taking dictation from John Sumner.

John Sumner rarely took to advertising his tea in the local newspapers. He was more likely to use hand bills, display material in shops, as well as the packet itself to carry leaflets offering goods at reduced prices to his customers.

A few of these early leaflets of Castle Street days still exist. Number 277 is for an aluminium tea strainer. Offer 312 was for the Patent Self-Straining 'Typhoo' Tea Pot at 9*d* (4½p) or a complete tea set in Longport Ware on ivory ground, banded with gold and deep sage green. Each of the items cost 9*d* (4½p) plus postage and the relevant 'Typhoo' packet fronts.

Clara Edith Simister in 1907, three years before she joined the firm.

'Sim' remembers John Sumner as a 'lovely man – a gentleman'. She typed his letters on an Olivetti typewriter. Her first Christmas box from 'Typhoo' shortly after starting was a ¼-lb packet of tea, which she took home to her mother. She stayed with the company for 27 years.

An early sales offer.

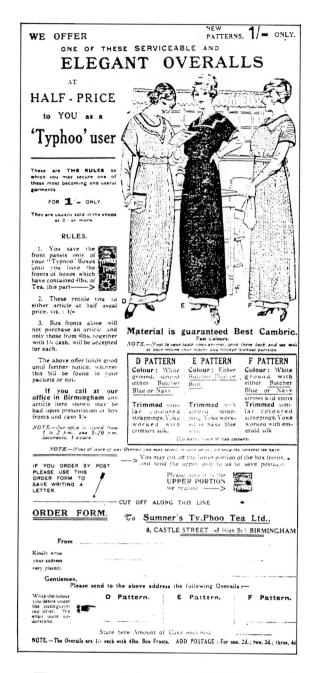

There was a choice in offer 313 between three different overalls at 1s (5p) each, while offer 314 was for the Royal 'Typhoo' Tea Tray measuring 12 in. by 15 in. The *Sutton Times* reported on 26 June 1914 that the King and Queen, whilst visiting the factory where they were made, selected for themselves a beautiful mahogany tea tray such as the one on offer by 'Typhoo'.

When the editor of the *Daily Chronicle*, the Hon. Rollo Russell, in 1914 attacked excessive tea drinking as causing more widespread damage to the nerves, digestion and general well-being

A series of sales promotion items offered by Typhoo pre-First World War.

PURE ALUMINIUM TEA STRAINERS.

USERS OF "Typhoo-Tipps"

MAY HAVE ONE OF THESE
PRETTY AND USEFUL ARTICLES
AT A NOMINAL PRICE.

THE USUAL
SHOP PRICE IS
4d. EACH.

BUT TO USERS
OF TY.PHOO
1½d. EACH ONLY.

HOW YOU MAY OBTAIN AT THE REDUCED PRICE
IF YOU CALL AT OUR OFFICES.

THE COUPON IS THIS PART OF THE BOX.

ALL YOU HAVE TO DO IS—Just to bring the front panel from a ½-lb. packet or two ¼-lbs.

This coupon, presented, will entitle you to the pure Aluminium Tea Strainer for the nominal price of **1½d.**

NOTE,

If you call at our office.

We close from 1 to 2;
at 5-20 daily,
and at 1 o'c on Saturday.

IT'S USES.

The Aluminium Tea Strainer may be used in two ways:—

1. Held over the cup when pouring out, it will catch any of the small leaf escaping through the spout.

2. To make an occasional cup of tea—place the leaf in the strainer, and the strainer upon a warmed cup. Fill it to the top with freshly boiled water, cover with a saucer; allow to stand from 5 to 10 minutes.

NOTE.—No harm will ensue from long standing as the injurious crude tannin found in ordinary tea is not present in "Ty.phoo-Tipps."

A FURTHER WORD ABOUT THESE STRAINERS.

The Aluminium of which they are made is particularly pure metal; white and bright, it will clean like silver. It will never rust and will retain its freshness for years.

IF YOU WISH THE STRAINER SENT BY POST
FILL IN AND SEND US THE ORDER FORM BELOW.

ORDER FORM.

TO Sumner's Ty.Phoo Tea Ltd.,
8, CASTLE STREET (off High St.) BIRMINGHAM.

From _____

kindly write
your address
very plainly.

_____

_____

Gentlemen,

Please send to the above address, post paid, a Pure Aluminium Tea Strainer for which I enclose, as a coupon, the front panel of a half-pound packet of Ty.phoo and stamps value 2d.

In 1914 'Typhoo' put into their packets coloured cards of British birds and their eggs for customers to collect. There were twenty-four cards altogether, each card depicting a different bird. Cards for collecting in sets proved very popular and were included in the packets for many years.

65

than any other single factor in England, alleging it hurt the heart, produced rheumatism and hindered growth, 'Typhoo' were quick to turn this to their advantage. They put out a leaflet pointing out that tannin was the offender and that 'Typhoo' leaf-edge tea was devoid of tannin. For their health's sake, the leaflet advocated people should turn to 'Typhoo' Tea.

John Sumner was always aware that others might try to take advantage of his promotion of leaf-edge tea, a word he coined and was ready to defend. Since the introduction of 'Typhoo' Tipps tea, some people had imitated the word 'Tipps', unaware that the extra 'p' was the result of a printer's error. In 1916 he complained that another tea company, which today is a major name in the trade, was advertising leaf-edge tea and including in their advertisements statements lifted from 'Typhoo's' own leaflets. His response was to send out a circular to all medical men on the books stating that the competitor's tea was not leaf-edge but in fact small Broken Pekoe containing 9.5 per cent tannic acid. His appeals were supported by the Chamber of Commerce who approached the other company requesting they desist.

In July 1916, Bromley & Co. were given notice to vacate the ground floor of 8 Castle Street by September 1916, making available much needed space for expansion. The directors had been debating as to whether they should install their own blending machinery which at this point in the company's development they felt might result in an appreciable economy. Before taking any action, however, they would first await a reply from their Ceylon agents as to what terms they would charge in future for buying without blending. According to the minutes of a meeting of the directors on 11 October 1916, the response of the agents was 'vague and unsatisfactory'. All thoughts of installing blending equipment at Castle Street were shelved for the time being.

The problem of obtaining electric power from the Corporation was finally resolved when the Birmingham Electricity Department consented to a six-electric-horsepower supply being laid on.

At the annual meeting of shareholders in 1916 J. H. Brindley acted as chairman, also present were John Sumner, managing director, J. R. Hugh Sumner (his son), director, Mrs J. Sumner, preference shareholder, whilst Mr Alfred Tustain represented Ault & Co., Auditors. Mr C. E. Packe was secretary. Net profit for 1916 was reported as £2,903 8s 9½d.

In March 1917, Ceylon exchange control difficulties resulted in shipments being delayed and production was threatened. 'Typhoo' was forced to resort to the London market but found

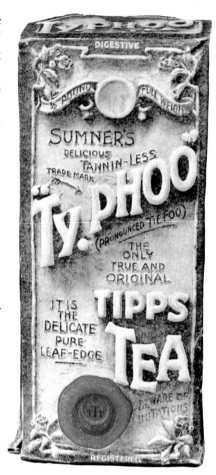

'The only true and original Tipps Tea'.

The reverse of this First World War ½-lb packet explains just how economical is 'Typhoo Tipps' leaf-edge tea.

prices dearer and was obliged to raise the price from 2s 10d to 3s (15p) per pound. Only one month later the price had again to be raised to 3s 2d per pound.

The most serious threat to the 'Typhoo' business since the bank had called in the overdraft in 1905 occurred in March 1917. Under the exigencies of war, the government decreed what was known as 'The Tea Control', under which all tea was to be bought up and then rationed out to the trade at one uniform price. As 'Typhoo's' trade was based solely on Ceylon leaf-edge tea, ordinary tea would not do, and if they were not allowed their special tea they would be ruined.

Companies were required to provide by a certain date the names and addresses of their retail trade customers together with the quantity required each month. This would then be allocated and supplied by the government.

'Typhoo's' protests fell on deaf ears and they were told they would get their supplies like the rest. In spite of interviews with heads of governmental departments and support by various Members of Parliament, their requests for supplies of leaf-edge tea were turned down.

Even an appeal signed by 4,000 medical men sent to the government met with the same negative response. As a last resort 'Typhoo' appealed to the public for their support. A circular was inserted into every packet of tea sent out asking the recipient to write personally to the Tea Controller requesting a continuance of 'Typhoo's' leaf-edge tea, stating particularly the reason for which his or her doctor had prescribed it.

Having done as much as they were able, the directors of 'Typhoo' could only wait. Two weeks had passed when a letter was received from the Tea Controller stating that he was being plagued by correspondence from customers of 'Typhoo' and it must stop. Another ten days passed when a more strongly worded letter from the Controller was received demanding the deluge of letters which were still flooding in be stopped immediately because they were hampering the work of the department. 'Typhoo's' answer was that it was beyond their powers.

Then came a summons to attend at the Tea Controller's office in London. An interview with the heads of the department followed after which the permit was granted. Their objective achieved, all at 'Typhoo' gave a sigh of relief.

Only three days remained to send out and get back signed indents from the company's 6,000 agents, of whom about half were chemists. After feverish activity, the forms were sent out – but only 3,000 came back in time; the remainder would, through their delay, go without their 'Typhoo' tea until after the war.

Armistice Day, 11 November 1918, was a joyous one for the

S.O.S. ! ! !

To the Users of "Ty.phoo" Tea

YOU ARE IN GRAVE DANGER

OF HAVING

Your Supplies of "Ty.phoo" Tea Cut Off

UNDER THE FOOD CONTROL

You can help to avoid this.

There is no exaggeration in the above heading, for by the new Food Control regulations private importation of tea by licence, as hitherto, is to be stopped. The Government is proposing to buy all tea abroad and to distribute t to merchants throughout the Kingdom in equal proportions.

On the face of it this seems good, and in view of the present shortage, if we dealt in ordinary tea, it would be quite fair.

are not allowed to continue to import our special leaf-edge tea.

We ask you to write a Letter.

In order to prove to the Food Controller how many people are affected if "Ty.phoo" tea supplies stop, we ask you in your own interests to write a letter to :—

J. R. CLYNES, Esq., M.P.,
Parliamentary Secretary, Ministry of Food,
House of Commons,
LONDON, S.W. 1.

stating in as few words as possible

1. That you are a user of "Ty.phoo" leaf-edge tea.

2. That you hear the Company's licence to import their tea is in danger of being suppressed.

3. That as you can use no other, you would consequently be totally deprived of tea in that event.

4. If you have been ordered "Ty.phoo-Tipps" by your Doctor or Nurse, say so, giving his or her name, and state for what ailment you take it.

5. End by saying that you beg of the authorities to see that the "Typhoo" Company's licence to import may be continued.

How the Scheme would hit you.

But, if our licence is not continued, we should not be able to secure the practically tannin-free tea which we provide for the use of Invalids, and those who, with weak digestions, cannot take ordinary whole-leaf tree.

Owing to the shortage of tonnage, due to U-boat sinkings, everyone will have to be rationed in tea, and as to this, users of "Ty.phoo" will patriotically and cheerfully fall into line ; but when they find, that unlike others, they will get no tea at all, as they cannot drink the ordinary, they will have just cause for complaint.

We are appealing to the Ministry.

On your account, as well as our own, we are asking that our licence to select and import our special tea in Ceylon may be continued. We do not ask for more than our proper proportion of tea : you would not wish us to do so. We do not ask to be free from Control as to price. But we do ask that you may not have to go without tea, and that our business may not be closed down, seeing the ordinary tea would be of no use to you or to us.

This is how you may help.

The Food Controller is, under great difficulty, endeavouring to do his best for the people as a whole, but unless it can be proved to him that there does exist a large section to whom ordinary tea is injurious, and that great numbers are taking "Ty.phoo" under doctors' orders, he naturally will not realise that you are under any special hardship, as you will be, if we

That " God helps those who help themselves " is as true as it ever was. So don't delay !

WRITE YOUR LETTER NOW please, and POST IT TO-DAY.

SUMNERS *Typhoo* TEA LIMITED.
HEAD OFFICE. (FOR ALL CORRESPONDENCE)
CASTLE ST. BIRMINGHAM.
LONDON { CLEARING OFFICE : LLOYDS AVENUE HOUSE : E.C.
BONDED STORES : COMMERCIAL ROAD : E.

Telephone : Birmingham Central—1343
" London Avenue—1672
Telegraph : "Ty.phoo" Birmingham.
" "Typhootico" London.

JOHN BELLOWS, GLOUCESTER 1917

(476)

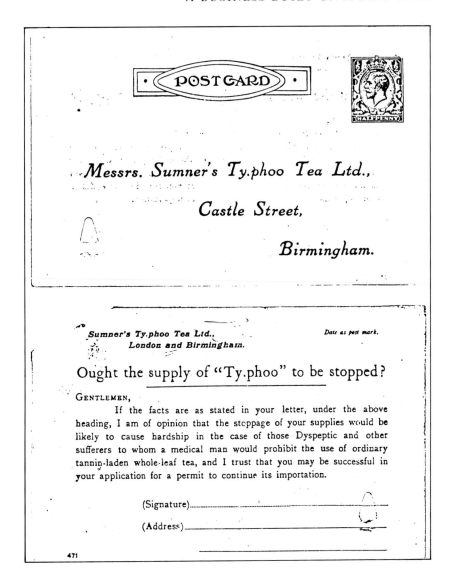

POSTGARD

½ HALFPENNY

Messrs. Sumner's Ty.phoo Tea Ltd.,

Castle Street,

Birmingham.

Sumner's Ty.phoo Tea Ltd.,
London and Birmingham.

Date as post mark.

Ought the supply of "Ty.phoo" to be stopped?

GENTLEMEN,

If the facts are as stated in your letter, under the above heading, I am of opinion that the stoppage of your supplies would be likely to cause hardship in the case of those Dyspeptic and other sufferers to whom a medical man would prohibit the use of ordinary tannin-laden whole-leaf tea, and I trust that you may be successful in your application for a permit to continue its importation.

(Signature)_____

(Address)_____

471

Thousands of copies of these appeals inundated the Ministry's offices in London. It did the trick and Typhoo's Special Leaf-edge tea supplies were restored.

whole nation. It was also a day tinged with sadness, because the company secretary and commercial manager, Charles E. Packe, who had been so actively involved in the struggle with the Tea Controller, died of pneumonia after having contracted influenza. He was succeeded as company secretary by Captain P. G. F. Parker.

With hostilities at an end, 'Typhoo' anticipated the relaxation of tea controls within the next few months by instructing their Ceylon agents to buy 500 chests of leaf-edge tea and to hold them until able to ship. They were anxious to prepare their pipeline at the earliest possible moment and to pre-empt any sudden demand.

TY·PHOO

5. Entrepreneur

As soon as it was announced in March 1919 that tea controls were at an end, 'Typhoo' prepared a circular to be sent to the 3,000 agents who had failed to indent, asking them to re-open their accounts. By the evening only three hundred circulars had been posted. The following day when the staff arrived at work prepared to send off the remaining circulars, they were surprised to find in the morning's post a great batch of orders from lapsed agents who had been quick off the mark as soon as controls had ceased. Having been deprived of their 'Typhoo', their customers were now clamouring for it. So great was the congestion of orders that no more circulars were sent out while every effort was made to clear the backlog.

It soon became evident that only a few agents had been lost. So great was the demand for 'Typhoo' the year following the lifting of the controls that the company was hard pressed to meet demand and extra staff was taken on.

One person who started at 'Typhoo' in 1919 was fourteen-year-old Edith Grainger, now Mrs Shutt. She recalls that Castle Street was very narrow and the works old and dilapidated. A clocking-in clock stood at the top of the stairs letting out a loud clung as each card was stamped with the time. The cloakroom was very small and had a tap and sink close to where the hats and coats were hung. It was a regular occurrence for girls to find their hats floating in the sink.

All the girls were required to learn each other's job and always the first job was to stamp the price on the packet. There were only two lines working when Edith Grainger started, with about ten girls on each line. Two girls would carry sacks of tea to the attic and tip them into the hopper from where they would be gravity fed to the lines on the floor below. Sometimes a nail might get stuck in the hopper, bringing the whole operation to a standstill.

In the packing department one girl would make up the card-

Today in her eighty-third year, Edith Shutt explained how in 1919 when she was about to leave school, her mother saw an advert in their halfpenny 'Birmingham Mail' for packers at Sumner's 'Typhoo' Tea Ltd. She was allowed half a day off school on the Friday, was interviewed by the works manager, Mr R. H. Burton, and started work the following Monday morning at nine shillings a week.

board packet whilst another made the inner liner by wrapping a piece of paper round a block of wood and gluing the folded end. This was put into the packet and passed down the line where it was held under a chute and, when a pedal was pressed, a ¼ lb of tea dropped into the packet. After check-weighing it was passed on, then glued and sealed, being made up into a 5-lb parcel at the end of the line and stacked. Ten completed parcels were packed into an empty 'Typhoo' tea chest and sent down to the despatch department. The pedal-automatic machines enabled eight to ten packets to be filled per minute.

When Edith Grainger started in 1919 the packing-room was long and narrow, with Mr Burton's desk standing in a corner. Lighting was provided by gas mantle whilst heating consisted of overhead gas heaters and a coal fire. The task of lighting the coal fire would be delegated to a junior or newcomer. Orders for shops were packed in 5-, 10- and 20-lb parcels. If any girl was to deliver a parcel during her own time, she received 2½d.

If there were any special offers or promotions being made, then details were tucked into each packet before sealing. If a girl got any glue in her eye it was Edith's job to take the girl to the eye hospital for attention.

Chests of tea, on arrival at Castle Street, were accommodated in the basement where they would be opened with claw hammers. The girls were required to wear thick leather gloves which wore out quite quickly. To avoid unnecessary expenditure, all nails extracted during chest opening were re-used to seal packed stock in the 50-lb chests. If Mr Burton suspected a bent nail had penetrated a packet he would insist on the chest being re-opened and checked, much to the chagrin of the girls who were paid a bonus on the number of chests sealed.

From 1921 Miss E. Doolittle was the supervisor of chest opening. After she had been there for a while Mr Burton called all the girls together and told them that Miss Doolittle had been upset by girls making fun of her name so, from then on, she was to be known by her mother's maiden name of Miss Stokes.

On the ground floor was the despatch department where girls would lift 50-lb chests onto the LMS horse-drawn cart to be taken to the railway for distribution. Some customers would call in at Castle Street with their orders where Miss E. E. Akers, who was in charge of sales on the first floor, would attend to them.

The girls' welfare was the province of John Sumner and Richard Burton; the former in particular encouraged the girls to save at least one shilling a week (5p) out of their wages to buy savings certificates. Every August and Christmas, John Sumner gave the girls a bonus; in keeping with his ideas on thrift, the

R. H. Burton.

bonus was in the form of savings certificates. In 1920 he was to start an innovative scheme to distribute shares among employees. Over £300 of shares were distributed amongst twelve employees. Many more employees were subsequently issued with shares. John Sumner had always encouraged his girls to be thrifty and he felt the ownership of shares would give them an added interest in the progress of the company.

Canteen facilities consisted a small room with a table and bench where the girls would eat the food brought from home or from the little coffee-shop below in Castle Street. They were allowed a free cup of tea during breaks but were required to pay 2*d* a week for milk.

In the early days internal communication was by means of a speaking tube connecting the various floors. The person using it would blow down it to operate a whistle at the other end. After speaking down the tube it was then held to the ear for the reply. A telephone was later installed. When Edith Grainger started at Castle Street there were no lifts, these were to come later. Documents were passed from floor to floor in a box pulled up and down a shaft by a rope.

When 'Typhoo' first moved into Castle Street from their shop at Hutton House, High Street, they rented only the two top floors. As other tenants moved out so 'Typhoo' expanded until they occupied the whole building. Even this was not enough to contain such a rapidly growing company and when in 1918 Sir William Avery's Birmingham estate came on to the market John Sumner was quick to grasp the chance of purchasing the freehold building adjoining the works.

In October 1919 the death was announced of Mr J. H. Brindley, who was not only a director of Sumner's 'Typhoo' Tea Ltd and long-time friend of John Sumner, but had also founded The Priory Tea and Coffee Co. Mr Alfred Tustain, accountant with the firm Ault & Co., was chosen as his successor on the board. His appointment commenced on 1 November 1919 with the additional duties of secretary. Three months later a full-time company secretary was employed, Mr Roland Record.

On 4 December at a meeting of the directors it was announced that the capital of the company was to be increased to £100,000 by the creation of 8,500 £1 B preference shares and 89,500 £1 ordinary shares. In January 1920, John Sumner was pleased to be able to report that the company was making satisfactory progress. By April there was a healthy £10,525 cash balance in the bank and stocks of tea stood at £46,000. February had seen the purchase of three automatic weighing machines from the firm of Southall & Smith of Hockley, Birmingham at the cost of £140 each. That same month the price of 'Typhoo' had been

'What struck me most,' wrote Mr Roland Record shortly after joining the company, 'perhaps was the remarkable ease with which everything seemed to go – the rhythmical swing of it all. For instance, in other big houses with which I had been associated, business was intermittent, rushes and quiet times with a feverish scramble for orders in which estimates and contracts played an important part. Here was nothing of these; the demand I found was uniform and continuous. The orders apparently streamed in of their own accord. By every post they arrived in shoals. Only a few men scattered over the country opened new agencies, which then carried on automatically.'

raised by *2d* to *3s 6d* (17½p) per lb, only to be reduced by *2d* seven months later.

Privately purchased teas imported into the country for the account of 'Typhoo' were required to be cleared through Customs and placed into bond until needed for use. As John Sumner did not, at that time, have the facility of his own shipping department in Birmingham, he employed the services of a London firm, R. M. Holborn & Sons, who were buyers and blenders in their own right, to effect the necessary clearance and warehousing arrangements. This company was to become more closely associated with 'Typhoo' by subsequently becoming its London subsidiary. However, it was felt necessary to form a separate buying operation; in 1920 Tea Buyers came into existence, with offices located off Corporation Street. All purchases from then on were channelled through Tea Buyers in Birmingham.

John Sumner was ever on the look-out for means of increasing sales yet keeping to a minimum any administration costs. On 16 March 1920, he introduced a cash-with-order system, having first circularised all his agents offering larger discounts to those who would use the system. The response proved favourable and by the end of 1921 over 97 per cent of the 10,120 agencies had availed themselves of the system.

The company also benefited. Practically no book-keeping was required. No day books or ledgers were needed, only a combined loose-leaf sales and cash book with orders on one page and cash opposite. Orders received in the morning were practically all either ready to be despatched or actually sent out on the same day. Within four months the bank overdraft had been reduced by £18,000.

Miss Nelly Corbett, who started at the company in 1920, remembers it as a 'funny old building, very old. You went up a narrow staircase to the office which was a long narrow room with a high desk all down one side under the window overlooking Castle Street. Clerks sat on high stools. It was very Dickensian. There was an old-fashioned telephone and overhead were heaters with a hanging switch to work them.' It was she who had to answer that first telephone and, not being used to it, was terrified each time it rang. John Sumner, whose office was close to Miss Corbett's desk, would often come out and turn down the heaters if he thought it warm enough. She remembers John Sumner as being very paternalistic and always fair.

Everyone, including all the girls, were keen and interested in the weekly tea sales figures. Before the cash-with-order system, the books of account were kept meticulously by Miss Davis and Miss Hodson. All the heavy ledgers were kept in lockers in an upstairs room each night and each morning they were brought

Miss Ellen Corbett started at 'Typhoo' when she was fourteen years of age. She was interviewed by Miss J. Lucas, the office superintendent, for an office position. Most girls at the time started at ten shillings a week but she had asked for fifteen shillings and had been surprised to be given it. Together with a time-keeping bonus of 1s 6d (7½p) her earnings of 16s 6d (82½p) per week had made her feel quite wealthy.

She stayed with the company for forty-five years.

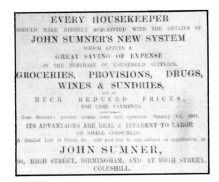

EVERY HOUSEKEEPER
SHOULD MAKE HERSELF ACQUAINTED WITH THE DETAILS OF
JOHN SUMNER'S NEW SYSTEM
WHICH EFFECTS A
GREAT SAVING OF EXPENSE
IN THE PURCHASE OF HOUSEHOLD SUPPLIES.
GROCERIES, PROVISIONS, DRUGS,
WINES & SUNDRIES,
AND AT
MUCH REDUCED PRICES,
FOR CASH PAYMENTS.
JOHN SUMNER'S present system came into operation January 1st, 1881.
ITS ADVANTAGES ARE REAL & APPARENT TO LARGE
OR SMALL CONSUMERS.
A detailed List of Prices, &c., sent post free to any address on application to
JOHN SUMNER,
98, HIGH STREET, BIRMINGHAM, AND AT HIGH STREET,
COLESHILL.

John Sumner's father had operated a similar cash-with-order system some forty years before, as seen in this advertisement from the 'Coleshill Chronicle' of 22 January 1881.

down by the office juniors. Miss Corbett remembers a little trap at the end of the sales office where Miss Akers would serve customers. At the end of the long room was a small kitchen where girls would heat up their dinners on a gas stove. All girls were expected to leave once they got married – although this rule was later relaxed.

Teas imported into the country for 'Typhoo' came in through the ports of London, Liverpool, Manchester and Avonmouth. Deliveries to Birmingham from bonded warehouses came by road, rail and, it seems, by canal, for a record dated 31 January 1922 shows stocks of tea in Birmingham:

Fellows Moreton's Warehouse	1,826 half chests
On canal	476
Our basement	629
Packed	850
	3,781

A new ¼ lb packing machine was ordered in November 1922, costing £175. Such had been the continuing growth of the company that the Castle Street works were full to capacity of machinery and hands. Talk of extensions to alleviate the over-crowding began in July 1923 after factory inspectors had pointed out that, unless more cubic space was found, the company would be infringing the rules.

As 'Typhoo' still owned land adjacent to Castle Street works, plans were drawn up to erect further extensions. The new extension had literally just begun in August 1923 when it was summarily halted; it had been drawn to John Sumner's attention that, a short distance away in Bordesley Street, a large building which had been used as saw mills and depots now stood vacant and was up for sale.

The directors visited the site and, in Ronald Sumner Kneale's words:

> Upon inspection we found ourselves first upon the ground floor in a great square, empty, echoing place, considerably larger than the interior of the Birmingham Town Hall, a little dangerous by reason of the yawning sawpits on all sides, for it had been erected some 25 years earlier and since used by a large firm of timber importers. Three rows of iron pillars – 25 in all – supported the floor above. 'What a place for a bonded stores!' remarked one of our directors.

They made a rough measurement – 50 yards by 32 yards, 14,400 square feet – and estimated a storage capacity at over 20,000 chests of tea. While the ground floor would provide a possible bonded warehouse, the floor above had great potential for pack-

Christina Fryer joined the company in 1922 at the age of fourteen and stayed for forty-six years. She started in the packing department stamping prices on the packets and remembers those early days before automatic machines when the whole packing operation was carried out by hand and a foot pedal was used to deliver a ¼ lb of tea into the packet. She remembers a form of blending with the girls tipping numbered sacks of tea into one of the four corresponding sections of the hopper. Occasionally a sack would be inadvertently dropped into the hopper bringing production to a grinding halt much to the embarrassment of the red-faced girls.

The Castle Street premises in the 1920s.

At the Kinver terminus of the Kinver Light Railway. Typhoo's first tram advertising appeared on trams in the Black Country. The driver and conductor frame two of the earliest 'Typhoo' Tipps adverts.

ing and despatch purposes. But perhaps the greatest attraction of the site was the fact that it had its own private dock connecting with the London, Liverpool, Manchester, Bristol and Birmingham Canal.

The Canal Wharf, known as either Bangor Wharf or Bordesley Street Wharf, had previously housed Knight and Gossling, timber merchants in the 1860s, ten coal merchants, as well as Robert Beddell, Agent and Machine Clerk to the Birmingham Canal Company until the late 1880s. His successor, Henry Hewlett, and four remaining coal merchants were there in 1924 when 'Typhoo' possessed the building vacated by Tailby & Co. Ltd, Timber Merchants.

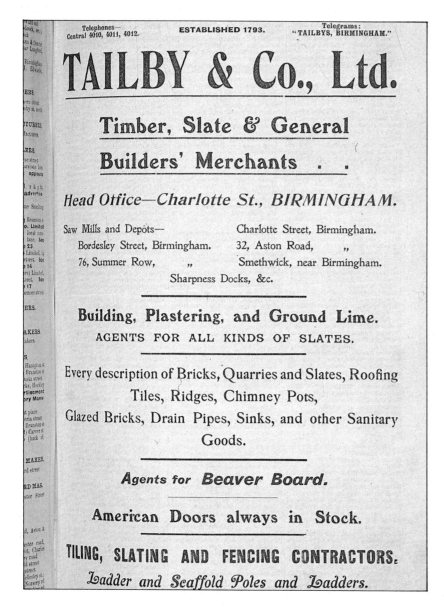

An entry in Kelly's 'Directory', 1918, by Tailby & Co. Ltd, the previous occupants of the Bordesley Street building.

All the directors were in agreement that the building, known as the Bangor Wharf Saw Mills, would be a suitable acquisition, ideally suited for housing packing and despatch works in addition to providing the company with its own bonded warehouse in Birmingham. But before they went ahead with the purchase, they first had to obtain permission from the Customs and Excise to operate it as a bonded warehouse. On 14 September 1923 the following entry appeared in the company's Minute Book:

> A letter dated 10th September 1923 was received from the Customs & Excise Office in Birmingham stating they are prepared to give favourable consideration of our application for provisional approval of the ground floor of the proposed premises as a Bonded Warehouse for dry goods upon certain conditions when the premises have been acquired by us.

Having been given provisional approval they approached the owners of the building over the purchase price. An entry in the Minute Book on 11 October 1923 records:

> Resolved that the building known as the Bangor Wharf Saw Mills be purchased by the Company for use as a Bonded Warehouse & packing Works at the price of £2750 as agreed upon with the Vendors, The Butchers Hide Skin & Wool Co. Ltd., New Canal Street, Birmingham.

Shortage of space had led 'Typhoo' to negotiate with LMS for 100 square yards, storage at Curzon Street, but once the new building had been completely brought up to standard, the company would need neither outside warehouses nor the London bonded warehouse in Commercial Road.

'Typhoo' could well afford the new building and all the renovations without having to approach their bank for a loan. The annual accounts for 1923 reveal the financial soundness of the company:

	£	s.	d.
Castle Street Premises	Freehold		
Barclays Bank	61,794		
Investments	105,717	2	7
Sales of Tea	632,900	1	7½

In the meantime 'Typhoo' accepted an offer on 6 November 1923 from John Goodman & Sons to purchase the freehold works at numbers 5, 6 & 7 Castle Street for the sum of £7,000. On 24 December it was resolved to sign an underlease on the Bordesley Street premises dating from 25 March 1923 for 66 years. An offer of £2,000 in February 1924 was accepted from J. G. Hammond & Co. Ltd for property at 12, 13 and back of 14 and 15 Castle Street.

Architects drew up plans and estimates for work and plant

John Sumner's nephew, Ronald Sumner Redfern Kneale, started with the company in August 1922. He was the son of Mary Augusta, who had first suggested that John Sumner sell the small-leafed tea that she liked in his shop, little realising the chain of events this would lead to in time.

Ronald was an engineer and was to prove a valuable asset to the firm. As John's own son, J. R. Hugh Sumner, did not at this stage take an active part in the company, preferring farming, Ronald Sumner Redfern Kneale helped to provide the family involvement. This he did to good effect as general manager and favourite of all the girls, being tall and good looking. He retired in 1948.

A bird's eye view of the Bordesley Street premises in 1926.

installations were obtained. John Sumner placed the responsibility for arranging, supervising and installing the new works with his nephew and general manager, Ronald Sumner Redfern Kneale. A contract was signed in February with Jeffreys & Sons Ltd for the alterations and additions to the Bordesley Street premises.

When work commenced the saw pits were filled in and a solid reinforced concrete foundation was laid, then a fine ferro-granolithic surface covered the ground floor. The packing and despatch floor above was strengthened and reinforced with expanded metal and levelled to take the packing machinery.

On completion in 1925 the factory would be equipped with the most up-to-date electrically driven machinery. There would also be a fine bonded store supervised by a resident customs officer who, in conjunction with Mr Leonard Goode, would check the movement of tea into and out of bond ensuring the relevant duty was paid. Once the bond was in operation, 'Typhoo' would draw out and pay duty on only that tea required immediately for blending whereas, with teas drawn from London bond, duty would be paid but it might be some time before the full quantity was used. The new operation would make more economic use of the company's funds.

Although the building was being fitted out with the most modern machinery, no provision was made to install blending equipment. All blending was still to be carried out by the Ceylon agents in Colombo which represented a considerable saving in labour and cost.

JOHN SUMNER & SON.

This ornately carved wooden shop sign with gold lettering had originally adorned the Bull Ring Shop. It was fixed to the wall of the staircase at the entrance at Bordesley Street and became a familiar sight to the many employees and visitors. Today it is displayed at Moreton, Merseyside, where the present 'Typhoo' packing works are situated.

In July 1931 Alfred Tustain, who had worked for the company on a part-time basis, made arrangements to devote practically the whole of his time to the business of 'Typhoo' as managing director.

With most of the tea forwarded to Birmingham by canal, teas were delivered from the vessels' sides in barges holding between 250 to 400 chests, direct into 'Typhoo' works. Each weekly shipment from Ceylon consisted up to 3,000 chests resulting in a regular convoy of barges proceeding up the Warwick Birmingham Canal, then into the Digbeth Branch, finally arriving at Bordesley Street. Discharge was safely effected under a covered shed during all weathers. Chests were lifted on an electric elevator to a gravity roller down which the chests ran to the bond 40 yards away.

The storage and movement of chests, packed stock and materials was revolutionised by the introduction of what was then called 'the portable platform' – today known as the pallet – which was moved about with a hand-operated truck that lifted the pallet clear off the ground. There were over 1,000 pallets in use in the factory, each carrying fifteen chests of bulk tea or 1,000 lbs of packed stock.

While Castle Street girls would take sacks of tea up to the hopper using a lift, at Bordesley Street the newly opened chests could be tipped into a magnetised sifter which removed paper and nails, and from here an 'endless band and bucket elevator' carried the loose tea to a hopper with a capacity of 1½ tons situated in a tower. The tea fell by gravity to a band conveyor, then to a battery of automatic weighing machines where teams of girls filled the packets and made up 5-lb parcels containing either ¼-lb or ½-lb packets. The palletised load of 1,000 lbs was then wheeled away to despatch.

A kitchen, canteen, rest and recreation rooms for women and girls were incorporated into the new building for the benefit of the workforce. The cloakroom, fitted with a locker for each girl and heated by hot water pipes, was a far cry from the Castle Street cloakroom where the girls had often retrieved their hats from floating in the sink. Today when some of the retired 'girls' reminisce, they speak fondly of the time spent at Castle Street, in spite of its many inconveniences.

Production and despatch were the first sections to move to Bordesley Street; the offices and sales were to remain at Castle Street until such time as a new extension was built to accommodate them.

Day-to-day business carried on with as little interruption as possible, during the move. An entry in the Minute Book on

13 March 1924 shows that an order had been placed for 10½ million insert cards on the theme of *Ancient & Annual Customs*. Also printed in 1924 for insertion were *Aesop's Fables* cards – coloured picture cards in a series of twenty-five which were keenly collected by users of 'Typhoo' tea. The following years saw numerous series of cards produced and many promotions launched.

"Ty.Phoo" Tea series of Æsop's Fables.

"Ty.Phoo" Tea, the tea that cannot cause indigestion.

"Ty.Phoo" Tea series of Æsop's Fables.

"Ty.Phoo" Tea will save you money and please you too.

"Ty.Phoo" Tea series of Æsop's Fables.

"Ty.Phoo" Tea, the all pure tea no stalk or stem.

"Ty.Phoo" Tea series of Æsop's Fables.

"Ty.Phoo" Tea, the tea so pure and yet so rich.

"Ty.Phoo" Tea series of Æsop's Fables.

"Ty.Phoo" Tea, the tea free from crude tannin.

"Ty.Phoo" Tea series of Æsop's Fables.

"Ty.Phoo" Tea, the tea free from crude tannin.

"Ty.Phoo" Tea series of Æsop's Fables.

"Ty.Phoo" Tea, the tea so pure and yet so rich.

"Ty.Phoo" Tea series of Æsop's Fables.

"Ty.Phoo" Tea, the tea that Doctors prescribe.

"Ty.Phoo" Tea series of Æsop's Fables.

"Ty.Phoo" Tea - One quality one price only.

"Ty.Phoo" Tea series of Æsop's Fables.

"Ty.Phoo" Tea is the tea with that nice nutty taste.

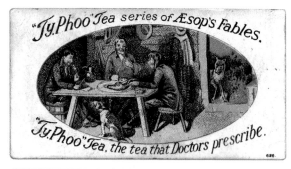

A 1924 beautifully illustrated set of Typhoo packet cards featuring Aesop's Fables. The reverse of each card carries the corresponding moral.

When the Ceylon agency agreement negotiated in 1909 by John Sumner was up for renewal in 1926, Alfred Tustain sailed out to Ceylon at the request of John Sumner to re-negotiate it and bring back the document containing the terms and conditions for John Sumner's approval and for the directors to add their signatures to those of the agent's directors. The finalised agreement was to run for fourteen years from 1 January 1926.

In 1926 the company proudly celebrated its 21st birthday. At

To celebrate the company's twenty-first birthday John Sumner arranged for the printing of 'The Story of "Typhoo"' containing articles by various members of the company relating to its history. The booklet was well received throughout the country by the trade and the company's 16,000 agents to whom it was dedicated.

the Annual General Meeting on 30 July 1926 John Sumner was pleased to announce that the new works had been 'running like clockwork for nine months' and that his son, J. R. Hugh Sumner, was to understudy him to the task of chairmanship and would in future be filling in his time partly in his business of farming and partly at 'Typhoo'. Having confounded all his early critics and doubters that his venture in 1905 would end in financial ruin, John Sumner was proud, twenty-one years later, to be the owner of such a successful firm that had given work to hundreds of people in Birmingham and Ceylon.

On 3 May 1926 a young girl, Edith Carey, joined the staff at Castle Street as a temporary clerk for one week. She was to stay for forty-two years. She well remembers the overhead gas heaters which would keep your head warm whilst your feet remained cold, and the tall stools and desks on which large ledgers were laid out. One of her duties was to look after the small switchboard that sat on the corner of her desk. Offices were still retained at Castle Street for John Sumner, his son Hugh and nephew Ronald Sumner Kneale.

Promotional ideas and schemes flowed from Roland Record's fertile mind. His *British Empire* picture cards in 1926 ran out sooner than anticipated. In October 1,000 glass plates for fixing to high-class grocers' windows were produced and in February 1927 *Robin Hood and His Merry Men* cards were hurried through. *The Animal Friends of Man* came from the printers in May 1927. In 1930 the *David Copperfield* series were so popular that a further four million had to be ordered. A doctor's meter-lamp scheme resulted in an additional 862 names being added to the medical persons list. At the end of the year it was proposed to print 100 million tramway tickets for advertising purposes. During 1928 the company's name was displayed on trams in Birmingham, Bolton, Bristol, Derby and Liverpool. In 1930 all 341 of Belfast's trams bore 'Typhoo's' advertisements.

The year 1927 also saw 'Typhoo' looking beyond British shores for sales, with a note in the Minute Book that all export prices were to be quoted FOB (free on board) English port.

Through John Sumner's influence ninety per cent of employees had joined the Savings Club; many also held shares and were in receipt of regular dividends as the company flourished. A suggestion box was set up on John Sumner's instructions as he always welcomed constructive ideas for improvements that would benefit both company and workers.

Having achieved success and prosperity, close to John Sumner's heart was the desire to give something back to society. He explained his wishes in a private letter to his son, J. R. Hugh Sumner, to be opened after his death:

> Continued acquisition of property, beyond the point of reasonable need, is not to be desired. This is why I have already disposed of much by way of philanthropy. And too, because I hold that if by industry, enterprise and sound management or good fortune, one succeeds in extracting much money from the Community, then a return of part by way of gratitude is only due.

With this in mind, in 1927 he derived much pleasure in founding the John Sumner Trust with £178,702 at its disposal of

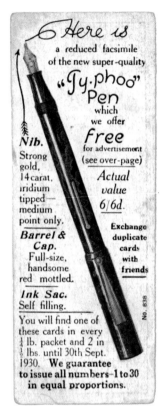

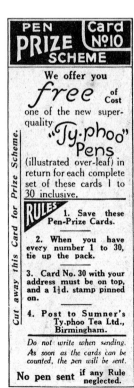

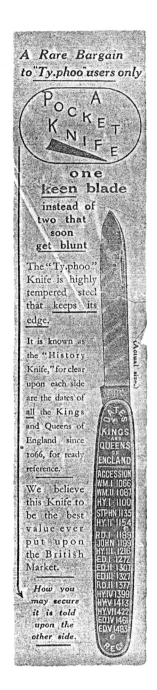

A Rare Bargain to "Ty.phoo" users only

A POCKET KNIFE

one keen blade

instead of two that soon get blunt

The "Ty.phoo" Knife is highly tempered steel that keeps its edge.

It is known as the "History Knife," for clear upon each side are the dates of all the Kings and Queens of England since 1066, for ready reference.

We believe this Knife to be the best value ever put upon the British Market.

How you may secure it is told upon the other side.

(Actual size)

DATES OF
KINGS
AND
QUEENS
OF
ENGLAND

ACCESSION
WM.I 1066
WM.II 1087
H.Y.I 1100
STPHN 1135
HY.II 1154
RD.I 1189
JOHN 1199
HY.III 1216
ED.I 1272
ED.II 1307
ED.III 1327
RD.II 1377
HY.IV 1399
HY.V 1413
HY.VI 1422
ED.IV 1461
ED.V 1483

A pocket knife printed with the dates of the Kings and Queens of England since 1066 was offered on 18 July 1928 for 1s 6d accompanied by two ¼ lb or one ½ lb packet fronts. One such knife was admitted recently by a Professor to have been of great assistance during school exams; he had kept his 'Typhoo' History Knife ever since.

which £132,686 was devoted to works and objects of philanthropy, public utility, education, literature, art, archaeology and research – excluding experiments involving animal suffering. Another £46,016 was to be used to aid, by annuity and otherwise, persons who either by ties of family or loyal service the founder conceived had claims upon him.

In 1930 he was to establish another charity, the Colehaven Trust and had erected in Coleshill some almshouses which today stand in Sumner Road, appropriately named after him. The Trust was established to benefit well-bred ladies of blameless character who found themselves in reduced circumstances, resulting in physical deterioration and an inability to cope. The Trust was inaugurated in March 1931.

In July 1928 it was proposed that an office extension incorporating a new boardroom be added to the Bordesley Street Works so that the staff from Castle Street could be installed there the following year. To meet the need for further extensions a 60¼ years' lease for additional land in Bordesley Street was obtained from the British Canal Navigation Company, commencing December 1928. A buyer was then found for the Castle Street property.

By April 1930 the move had taken place. The old Castle Street premises were entirely vacated and all staff transferred to the newly erected office and boardroom extension. On 28 April the first meeting was held in the new boardroom in Bordesley Street with the directors sitting at the table which John Sumner's grandfather, William, had bought on his marriage 110 years before. Special appreciation was conveyed by all members of the board to R. Sumner Kneale, general manager, for his very able and painstaking assistance to the architect Mr Weedon in carrying out the work involved in the extension. When on 22 April 1929 duty on tea was abolished, 'Typhoo' could reduce the price of its tea to the public by 4d per pound. A year later increased sales led to the Ceylon agents being instructed to purchase up to 10,750 half chests per month, thus ensuring a regular and steady pipeline of leaf-edge tea from Ceylon via the UK ports to the Birmingham works.

In accordance with company policy, J. R. Hugh Sumner sailed for Colombo in September 1929 to keep up the personal contact with the Ceylon agents. He was accompanied by one of the agents' directors, Mr C. S. Burns, who was returning to Ceylon after a holiday in England. He visited their offices in Queen Street, Colombo, the front door of which bore a brass plate proclaiming Sumner's 'Typhoo' Tea Ltd. He inspected the warehouses in Colpetty where bulk leaf-edge tea was brought for blending from public auctions or from tea gardens and where

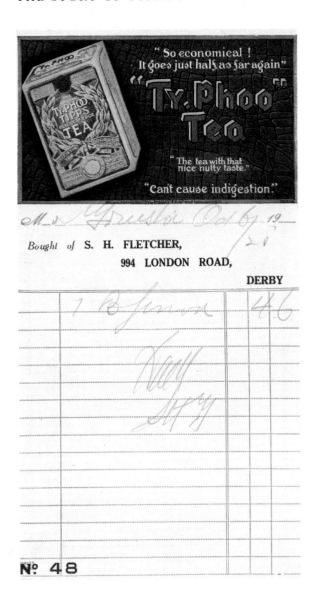

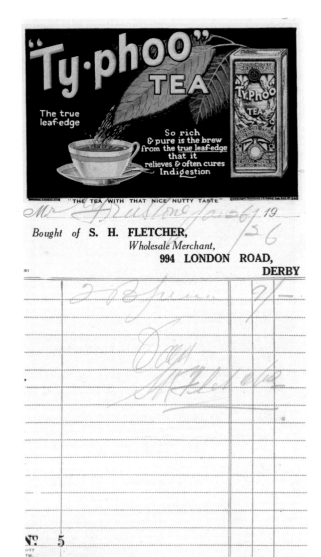

it was repacked into lead-lined, hermetically sealed chests hold-ing 70 lbs. The lead lining was eventually discontinued to be replaced by the now familiar aluminium foil and tissue paper. Having renewed contacts and settled any outstanding business, he returned home to England.

It was not long, however, before activities in Ceylon were causing concern in Birmingham. Although 1930 had seen increased profits with sales continuing to expand and the whole company now operating under one roof, all was not well with the quality of the leaf-edge tea (fannings) emanating from Ceylon. Unless action was quickly taken the company's reputa-tion and sales could seriously suffer.

The first person to indicate that anything was wrong was

A selection of grocers' receipt pads bearing 'Typhoo' advertisements during the 1920s.

The Almshouses at Coleshill supported by John Sumner's Trust.

S. W. H. Blake of R. M. Holborn & Sons Ltd. In addition to acting as 'Typhoo's' London tea buying and clearing agents, Holborns were also retained as tea consultants, tasting samples from shipments and blends as and when required. Mr Blake reported that shipment 69 had had a peculiar flavour and that shipment 70 had had something radically wrong – it was affected by damp or mould which had permeated the whole blend.

To compound 'Typhoo's' problems, the Birmingham Medical Officer of Health challenged their claim of being tannin-less, having analysed tea taken from a packet of 'Typhoo'. This allegation came as a shock to the directors who set about trying to refute it. Samples of 'Typhoo' were sent to experts at London and Birmingham Universities for analysis. They found a mini-

mal percentage of tannin present in the tea which although slightly higher than would normally be expected was still well below that found in other teas on the market.

Somewhat reassured by the universities' findings, the company still had the task of ensuring that future blends would conform to the expected 'Typhoo' standard. The following months saw a flurry of cables and letters to and from Ceylon. The Ceylon agents promised to investigate so as to discover the causes. In the meantime 'Typhoo' was able to buy their leaf-edge tea on the London market to make up the deficiency – but at higher cost.

For the rest of the year all shipments were monitored and still the quality was not fully up to requirements. Then in October 1930, a letter was received by Alfred Tustain, director of 'Typhoo', from an employee of the Ceylon agents expressing concern that 'Typhoo's' best interests were not being looked after by his employers; he had been ten years in charge of 'Typhoo's' bulking and blending and knew the reason for the deterioration in quality but dared not approach his employers for fear of losing his career. The reply from 'Typhoo' was that if he had any beneficial suggestions he should inform his principals.

This was followed by a further letter from Ceylon dated December 1930 the content of which came as a complete bombshell to the 'Typhoo' directors.

Being commission agents, the agents in Ceylon had agreed not to make a profit on the teas purchased but were supposed to

This shows the new office extension which was completed and put into use in 1930.

invoice 'Typhoo' at cost plus certain labour charges, adding commission. The letter received, however, implied a conspiracy amongst the agents' directors to the effect that large quantities of inferior teas were being purchased privately at a low price, put through rollers, and cut and sifted. Part of this was then disguised by mixing with genuine fannings and the price charged was greater than that paid at public auction. The remainder was sold to the Australian and American markets at a greatly reduced price, thus ensuring entry into those two markets from which they would otherwise have been excluded, with the whole operation being unwittingly subsidised by 'Typhoo'.

In addition to the 'cut' leaf included in the blend which had given rise to the tannin complaint, the agents were also including some private teas purchased cheaply from native traders in Colombo which, through poor storage, had acquired a baggy or musty taint and this had caused a deterioration in the whole blend. Having completed a blend, the agents would take the overall average price, which included good and overcharged poor quality teas plus a commission.

To back up his statement, the writer produced details of blends and prices which put beyond doubt the seriousness of the charges against his principals.

Armed with knowledge of the conspiracy and its mechanics, but not letting on, there followed a series of carefully worded cables with instructions to Ceylon designed to put a stop to the malpractice while causing considerable difficulty to the agents in continuing their Australian and American ventures at 'Typhoo's' expense.

Alarmed and puzzled by 'Typhoo's' strict instructions, which were obviously affecting their dubious operations, the agents continued to insist they be left to carry on as before – in the interests of 'Typhoo'.

During the first two months of 1931 matters showed no great improvement. On 3 March 1931 Ceylon agents were informed that J. R. Hugh Sumner and Alfred Tustain were sailing to Ceylon accompanied by Mr Blake, the tea expert from Holborns. On arrival at the Port of Colombo on 11 May they were met by two grim-faced directors who informed the party from Birmingham that their managing director, Mr Burns, had killed himself.

The outcome of tough discussions was a substantial payment to 'Typhoo' by way of compensation. The agency continued on an unsatisfactory basis for some time, finally terminating on 1 January 1933. On that date the newly appointed agents, Carson & Co. Ltd, took over the responsibility for buying and blending – a task which they carried out in a competent and proficient manner for many years until changing market trends led to less

Ceylon tea being required for the blends.

To cope with the increased buying on the London market and in order to house blending equipment over which the company could exercise control, additional land adjacent to the Bordesley Street works and offices was purchased in March 1932 from the Birmingham Canal Navigation Company Ltd for £4,106 10s 8d and a tender of £23,349 was accepted from Maddocks & Walford for the building extensions needed. Four years later a further 2,556 sq. yds of land were bought adjoining the Bordesley Street building and the acquisition in 1937 of another 830 sq. yds gave 'Typhoo' the opportunity to almost double the size of their premises. The contract dated June 1937 for extension number four by B. Whitehouse & Sons, Builders, for the sum of £52,989 would see the disappearance of two small cottages, numbers 66 and 98 Bordesley Street. A section of the canal basin would be filled in and covered by the new building which, when completed, would display across the top in gold letters: 'Typhoo' Buildings.

To the delight of everyone at 'Typhoo' on 3 June 1932 it was announced in the Birthday Honours List that a knighthood had been bestowed on John Sumner in recognition of his philanthropic services, amongst which was listed his founding of the John Sumner Trust and the Colchaven Endowed Homes for Gentlewomen, his interest in the work of the Voluntary Hospitals in Birmingham and District and his presidency of the General Hospital, of the Birmingham and Midland Counties Nerve Hospital and of the Bromsgrove Cottage Hospital.

Miss Nelly Corbett, who had been with the company since 1920, said of the day, 'I always remember the morning when Sir John was knighted. As he walked into the big general office, everybody stood up and cheered.' To celebrate the occasion a party was held for the employees and each received a bonus.

Sir John was now 76 years old and in declining health. His visits to the works were becoming less frequent although he still endeavoured to attend board meetings. His signature appears in the company's Minute Book for the last time on 28 July 1933. Three days later he attended his last Annual General Meeting, looking back with satisfaction at the progress made since starting in the rented top two floors in Castle Street in 1905, gradually taking over the whole building, extending, then purchasing premises in Bordesley Street, which itself had been so extended that the whole of the back land had been covered in. He also spoke of the new blending machinery of his own design, then being installed by Ronald Sumner Kneale.

Unable to attend a directors' meeting on 30 October 1933, the next was held in his home at Ham Hill, Powick, on 13 March

Sir John Sumner.

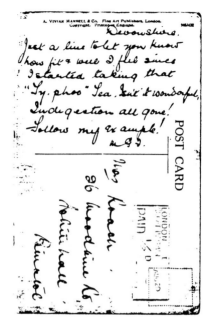

This wooden board greeted visitors at the bottom of the staircase at the Bordesley Street office entrance.

1934, during which a new director, Sebastian Hosgood, solicitor of Newhall Street, was appointed.

Sadly on 11 May 1934 Sir John Sumner, FSA, Founder of Sumner's 'Typhoo' Tea Ltd, died.

A special bus was hired to take employees to the service held at Coleshill Parish Church where he was interred in the family tomb. Each of the company's 346 employees benefited under Sir John Sumner's will.

Sir John Sumner would have appreciated this tribute to his leaf-edge tea expressed on a recently found post-card dated 29 August 1932:

> Just a few lines to let you know how fit and well I feel since I started taking that 'Typhoo' tea. Isn't it wonderful, indigestion all gone! Follow my example!

After the death of his father, J. R. Hugh Sumner was elected chairman with Alfred Tustain elected deputy chairman in addition to his office as managing director.

Two of the longest-serving members of staff on the books in 1934, apart from Mr R. Burton, works manager, whose time went back to the shop at 98 High Street, were Miss E. E. Akers, head of sales with nearly twenty-seven years' service and D. Riley, office supervisor with twenty-four years'. Miss Dorothy Davis, however, then had nearly eighteen years' service but was to go on to complete a record fifty years.

One newcomer was F. Parkin, who joined in February 1934 as works engineer just as the new blending plant, manufactured by Freys & Chalmers of Kent, was about to be installed. At that time about half the tea was purchased in London, the remainder from Ceylon.

Duty was still payable on tea which came in by barge straight into bond at Bordesley Street where Leonard Goode was foreman. Tea was packed by hand at six tables of twenty-two girls. The 70 lb tea chests had lead linings from which the lead was collected and sold. In December 1935 aluminium lining was tried out and in 1936 it permanently replaced the lead lining which was discontinued.

F. Parkin's first task was to build a conveyor to transport tea from the new blending plant to three huge bins in the packing works from where it was fed into automatic weighing machines which delivered either ¼ lb or ½ lb into packets held by girls seated at a long table. This table accommodated ten girls each side and two at the end. They filled the packets, inserted advertising material and sealed them at a rate of about 25–26 per minute.

A. J. Pendry had joined Holborns in 1926, becoming a taster, blender and buyer; he was seconded to Birmingham on a permanent basis when the new blending plant became operative. He set up the first tea-tasting department alongside the blending plant where the tea was tipped. After the war the tea department was to move to a small building at the rear of the factory alongside the canal.

Only when the blending machinery had been completely installed in 1934 were 'Typhoo' in a position to recruit their own resident tea taster/blender. Until then Mr Blake had travelled up by train from London to taste samples usually with Mr Alfred Tustain in attendance. Now they had only to look as far as Holborns in London to find a suitable person.

A. J. Pendry was joined at Bordesley Street by Mr A. L. Bayliss, also from Holborns, whose service was tragically short when in 1937 he collapsed and died while at work. His position was subsequently filled by 21-year-old E. H. Pedvin who had been well trained by Mr P. G. Simco, tea expert and buyer at Holborns. It was E. H. Pedvin who was to be summoned to Alfred Tustain's imposing office to be told, 'This is my son John. He's come to join us; take him downstairs and teach him something about tea.'

When the Budget of April 1936 imposed 2*d* per lb duty on the price of tea, this naturally affected the retail price. The 20,000 chests in 'Typhoo's' bonded warehouse were not sufficient to meet the rising demand and the company was obliged to hold additional tea in bonded warehouses at London, Liverpool, Manchester and Avonmouth.

The recently appointed Ceylon agents, Carson & Co., began to ship the teas they had bought to the UK via four ports: Liverpool saw 40 per cent of the trade, London 30 per cent, Manchester 20 per cent and Avonmouth 10 per cent. Over the years these proportions were to vary greatly. But it is noticeable that, of the eleven shipping lines specified to carry 'Typhoo' tea between 1933 and 1939, ten were British. During the first year the Bibby line carried 40 per cent – rising to 50 per cent by 1939 – whilst the other lines, City & Hall, Anchor & Brocklebank, Harrison, Glen, Nippon, P. & O., B. & I. and Blue Funnel were all to share the balance of cargo over the years.

F. Parkin, a marine engineer with a chief's ticket on the Blue Funnel Line who was later to be employed as works engineer, then works manager at 'Typhoo', recalls seeing hundreds of 'Typhoo' tea chests bound for England on the ships on which he served.

For some time 'Typhoo' tea had been shipped to Northern and Southern Ireland. On 26 November 1936 agreement was reached with Wynandy & Co. of Lausanne, Switzerland, to have bulk blended 'Typhoo' tea shipped from Ceylon direct to Switzerland, where 'Typhoo' tea cartons were to be printed for their use.

On 27 July 1938 it was announced that Alfred Tustain's son John would be joining the firm before the year was out. He was to go out to Ceylon to learn of conditions out there and then spend some time at the London subsidiary, R. M. Holborn & Sons, to familiarise himself with the markets. He left for Ceylon in January 1939, little dreaming that, two years later, he would be stationed there with the Royal Marines. The new extension was nearing completion and at the AGM the chairman, J. R. Hugh Sumner, announced another record profit at £399,960.

By the following year these profits had increased to £468,882 but the situation in Germany was worrying and the chairman was concerned about the possible implications for the rest of Europe and the UK. Profits could go on increasing only 'providing the Mad Dog of Europe and others in the Far East were muzzled'.

Having served the company since the early Castle Street days, Ronald Sumner Redfern Kneale was one of two additional directors appointed on 28 July 1939. The other was Roland Record, company secretary and architect of so many advertising and promotion schemes over the past years. To take over the responsibility for the publicity side, an advertising manager, W. J. Collins, had been appointed not long before.

Until the Second World War, packing was done by hand. Only the tea in ¼-lb and ½-lb quantities was automatically weighed before dropping into packets held by girls at the long tables. Tea chests continued to be opened by a hammer and hook until the 1960s when a cutting machine was introduced to remove the top of the chest, thus eliminating the sometimes hazardous task of releasing the lid by taking out the nails and tin staples.

Now the Ministry of Food became the owners of all stocks of tea, with a Tea Controller deciding the allocation to primary wholesalers. Swapping of teas allocated by the Tea Controller took place amongst companies. Four consignments – purchased for 'Typhoo' prior to the outbreak of hostilities but arriving in the UK after the Declaration of War – were commandeered by the Tea Controller but subsequently released a month later.

A consignment of 3,000 chests purchased on 13 September 1939 went down with the ill-fated SS *Yorkshire* when it was torpedoed in the Bay of Biscay on 17 October 1939. Export shipments direct from Ceylon to Switzerland and Barbados continued for a time until 1942 when a final entry in the Shipping

There is no information as to the origins of this pair of elaborately carved wooden replicas of the 1935 ¼ lb and ½ lb packet fronts. They evidently survived the damage to the buildings during the Second World War and came to light in the early 1970s.

Book recorded 100 chests bound for Knights Ltd, Barbados, on the SS *Bhima* as lost in action. Knights Ltd remains one of 'Typhoo's' oldest export customers.

Members of staff who were called to serve in HM Armed Forces were E. H. Pedvin, W. J. Collins and J. P. Tustain.

Rationing of tea became effective on 8 July 1940, each person being allowed two ounces. It was possible to save your ration and at any time within a four-week period obtain a ¼-lb packet. Tea was to remain on ration for the next twelve years, with the allowance fluctuating between 2 and 2½ ounces. It finally came to an end in October 1952, six years after the end of the war.

As has been mentioned earlier, in Chapter 3, it was not until 9 August 1940 that the first bomb fell on Birmingham, killing one man in Erdington and injuring several others. Mr F. Parkin attended this first incident. Now works manager, he was in a reserved occupation but had joined the Police Force in the mobile 'R' Division, being the proud owner of a new Hillman Minx car. He would transport policemen about on incidents until 6 am the following morning when he would go to work. Returning from one incident with three policemen in his car he pulled into the kerb as bombs fell all around, and immediately, the house outside which he had stopped received a direct hit. Debris came hurtling at, and through, the car; the glass shattered but by a miracle the only injury was a cut knuckle by one of the policemen. The following morning he drove his windowless car

Miss May Ward had joined the company as assistant secretary in 1924 and had been office manager at Bordesley Street until her marriage in 1939 to Alfred Tustain, deputy chairman and managing director, whose first wife had died some time previously.

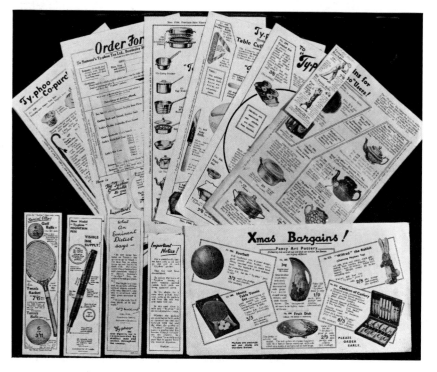

So many cards and inserts still exist that to cover all those issued over the years would need a separate book. For the discerning collector the publication 'Typhoo Tea Cards' compiled by Ian A. Laker, published in January 1976 by the London Cigarette Card Co., might be rewarding.

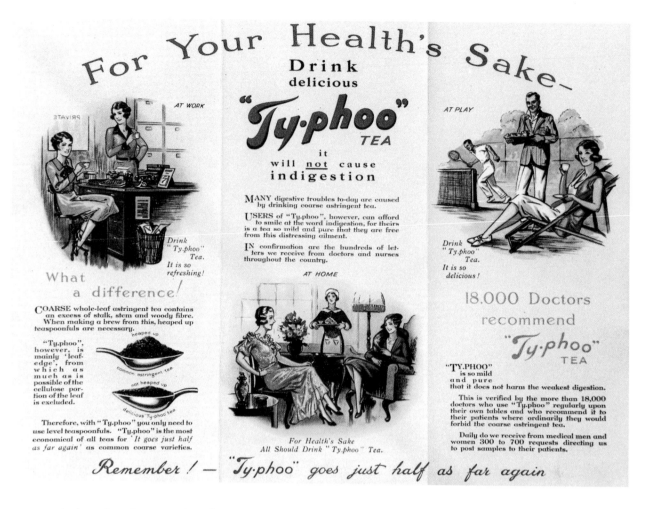

to work but in the evening it was pouring with rain, so he decided to leave it in the courtyard at 'Typhoo' Buildings, having pulled down the roller shutters to lock it in under the only overhead cover there. During that night a shower of incendiary bombs fell on 'Typhoo' but were extinguished by the sprinklers. However, one had fallen into the courtyard and had rolled under his beloved car. The next morning when he raised the shutters, he could not believe his eyes: his car was a burned-out shell. It cost him £2 10s to get it towed away and eventually he received £84 compensation.

A number of incendiary bombs fell on 'Typhoo' Buildings, including one in Roland Record's office, slightly burning a chair and causing minor damage before it and the others were quickly extinguished by the sprinkler system. Others fell in the main canteen and were similarly quickly doused.

On the night of the 9–10 April 1941 there was a very heavy raid on Birmingham when 250 raiders caused 1,121 casualties. In that raid bombs fell on the city centre causing severe damage

During the mid-1930s it was becoming increasingly difficult to obtain the full requirements of Ceylon fannings which had so long constituted the 'Typhoo' blend. When small quantities of Nilgiri tea were introduced, the description on the packet was changed to read 'An All Empire Tea'. Coming from southern India which has close geographical proximity to Ceylon, its characteristics were similar to Ceylon tea. Some carefully selected northern Indian teas were also included, but the blend still remained predominantly Ceylon, with only five per cent being Indian.

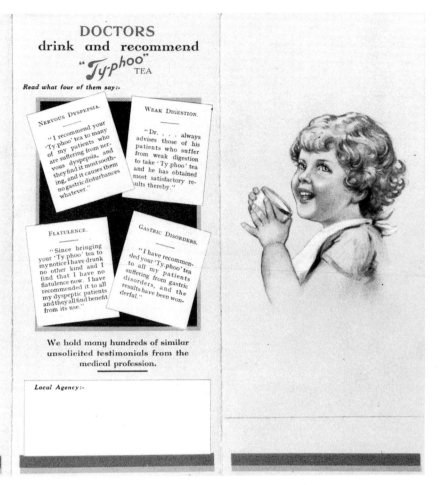

to property and, in the early hours of 10 April two bombs fell on 'Typhoo'. One landed at the rear of the Bordesley Street building between two of ten concrete-roofed brick air-raid shelters, each capable of holding twenty people, but fortunately empty; these completely disintegrated leaving a gaping crater. The other bomb scored a direct hit through the main canteen roof and floor bringing both down before a gigantic explosion ripped through the building, severing the sprinkler system and therefore allowing the resulting raging inferno to sweep unchecked through the factory, completely destroying it.

That morning, Miss Carey, who lived close to 'Typhoo' in Skinner Street, emerged with her mother from the Edgbaston Street air raid shelter. She saw a glow in the sky and said, 'It looks as if it could be "Typhoo".' As she and other weary employees made their way to work, treading carefully through a maze of criss-crossed hose pipes threading from Meriden Street into Bordelsey Street, they were met with a scene of complete devastation. All they could do was stand and stare in silence as

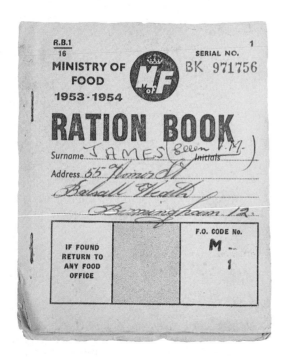

A Ration Book from the 1950s includes
tea coupons.

firemen trained their hoses on the inferno which they now had
under control. Water and tea combined, which under normal
circumstances would be complementary to each other, cascaded
down the front steps out of the factory into the street, swirling
across the pavement and rushing along the gutter in a brown
slurry to disappear down the drains.

Mr and Mrs Kneale were early at the scene doing their best to
help. Mrs Kneale, grimy and dishevelled in wellingtons and
waterproof clothing, handled some fire-fighting equipment. She
was, according to Miss Corbett, 'the John Bull sort'.

There was nothing anyone could do until the firemen had
finished their task and the situation could be assessed, although
it was quite obvious that with the works destroyed it would take
some time to recover. The girls were sent home and told to await
further instructions. The Ministry of Labour, however, wasted
no time and conscripted most of the girls into other jobs, leaving
about twelve to assist in the cleaning-up operation.

Temporary offices were set up at 21 Hermitage Rd, Edgbaston,
a building shared by another company. At Bordesley Street, all
available hands set to mopping up and clearing debris. In the
basement, the strong rooms were pumped free of water, leaving a
dirty oily stain to a height of about five feet up the walls. Until the
lifts were repaired, the only access to the strong rooms was by
way of a ladder. Once down there, a dank damp smell permeated
the air and, as the weather got warmer, flies began to swarm. The

This photograph owned by F. Parkin
shows the damaged roof of Bordesley
Street; the entire production area had
been destroyed during the night of
9/10 April 1941.

girls worked down here for three months, standing on wooden boards, wearing wellingtons, scrubbing clean all addressograph plates bearing agents' names and addresses so that messages could be sent explaining the situation and requesting details of their own records to replace those lost in the blaze. Some of the paper used to inform agents of the firm's plight was singed, bringing home to the recipient the reality of the predicament.

Some ladies who remained at 'Typhoo' during that most difficult period in the firm's history were Miss E. Isles, office manager, Miss D. Hodson, head cashier, Dorothy Davis, Connie (Stokes) Doolittle, who took over when Miss Akers left after thirty-four years' service in charge of sales, Nelly Corbett, Emily Bush, Hilda Browne, Edith Carey, Beryl Baker, Gladys Sturman and Christina Fryer, who became supervisor over the works after Miss Roe left.

Being unable to pack their own tea, 'Typhoo' made arrange-

The bomb entered through the main canteen, bringing down the roof and floor before exploding.

Tram 3 after having its windows blown out by a bomb blast at Miller Street Depot, April 1941. (From W. A. Camwell)

ments through Messrs Brooke Bond Ltd and Lyons Ltd – with the consent of the Ministry of Food – to have an 'Emergency Blend' packed. This generous action by the two companies was greatly appreciated by 'Typhoo'.

In May 1941, Alfred Tustain sent out a letter to the retail trade about the Emergency Blend, explaining that, as the works had been destroyed by enemy action, they would be unable to pack for an indefinite period.

One customer, Mr Pyle from Chichester, replied to Mr Tustain's letter on 14 June 1941:

> I regret to hear of your misfortune, at the same time, I have no desire to deal with the firms you mention. Kindly return cheque value £2-8-4*d* sent to you 31st March 1941

An appraisal of the situation revealed that the blending plant had escaped severe damage and that the three automatic packing machines acquired around the outbreak of the war were repairable in time.

Over 100,000 lbs of tea – which had been stored in huge bins – suffered smoke damage to varying degrees.

The services were obtained of a salvage crew from New Crane Wharf, all experienced tea warehousemen, whose work would take many months to complete. Fortunately some tea had been stored at outside warehouses although even this was vulnerable; on 10 May 1941, tea stored at the Monument Warehouses and the Red Lion Wharf Warehouse in London, was destroyed to the value of £10,215 19s 4d. When the salvage crew's work was completed, the total sum recovered from insurance and the companies department of the Board of Trade in respect of damaged tea, packing materials and coupon stock amounted to £56,884.

Great efforts were made by the remaining people at 'Typhoo' to create some semblance of order out of the chaos. By June 1941 Alfred Tustain was able to send out a letter announcing the repair of one of the three damaged automatic machines and the start of production, although on a reduced scale. For the time being, however, the sale of genuine 'Typhoo' tea had to be limited to a restricted area.

The first automatic packing machine purchased at the beginning of the war was, as recalled by Mr Parkin, from Job Days in Leeds. It would take a reel of paper and a stack of cartons, chop the paper off and form a bag around which the carton was also formed, filled with tea and delivered at a rate of 60 a minute. It needed only three girls to operate it. Eventually the other two automatic packing machines were brought into use and the

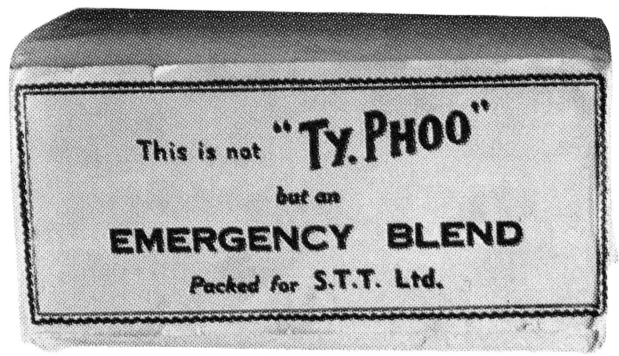

company was able to continue packing 'Typhoo' Tea without the need for outside help. A steady turnover of stock was maintained until the end of the war.

The 'Emergency Blend' packed by Brooke Bond and Lyons for 'Typhoo'; the tea was packed in paper, not the customary cardboard cartons.

Temporary single-storey warehouses were constructed alongside the arms of the canal, access being gained from Pickford Street. These were to remain until after the war when the damage sustained by the building could fully be repaired.

At a meeting of the directors on 1 September 1941 it was decided that, as the firm of R. M. Holborn & Sons, established since 1775, was now without income, it should be closed. On 29 September 1941, therefore, it was voluntarily wound up, with H. C. Kelley acting as liquidator.

It was on 1 December 1941 that the company decided on reconstruction; the name 'Sumner' was to be dropped and the new company, with a capital of £150,000, was to to be called 'Typhoo' Tea Ltd.

The wages book of August 1943 shows that a 14-year-old, working 47 hours a week, could expect to receive a wage of 19*s* 2*d* (96p) including 3*s* 2*d* (16p) War Bonus, whilst anyone aged 22 or over for the same hours received £1 18*s* 1*d* (£1.90) including a 6*s* 2*d* War Bonus.

The last siren of the war sounded in Birmingham on the night of 15 May 1944, although it would be another year before Germany surrendered, and three more months after that before the war with Japan ended.

TY·PHOO

6. Expansion and Merger

TEA rationing, which the Government had introduced in July 1940, ten months after the start of World War II, was in force throughout the nineteen forties. It eliminated commercial competition and the need to promote separate brands. It was a matter of the Government in the shape of the Ministry of Food ensuring that what small supplies were available were distributed as equitably as possible. The London Tea Auction Rooms remained closed. Supplies of tea were delivered to Bordesley Street by motor van, train and canal barge from the small depots which the Tea Controller had dispersed around Britain to reduce the likelihood of any one large supply being destroyed by the Luftwaffe.

With the war in Europe being over in May 1945 and in the Far East in August, the directors of Typhoo Tea Limited considered what form their advertising should take when they could return to the big spending they were accustomed to, aware however that Government regulations now prohibited them from recommending tea for its medicinal properties. To act as merchants in acquiring and dealing in the tea allocated by the Ministry of Food, they formed The Meriden Tea Company. With the grant which the Government gave them towards replacing buildings damaged in the war, they built a storage warehouse and a factory extension.

When the weekly tea ration was raised in December 1949 from two ounces per person to two and a half ounces, inevitably sales of Typhoo tea rose. It was an indication of what lay ahead, and the directors saw that they must act at once to raise the capital they would need to finance an enterprise capable of meeting the demands for tea which were bound to increase as the country returned to normality and shrugged off the austerity which was the price of victory. In March 1949, J. R. Hugh Sumner, chairman and his colleagues on the Board, opted for 'going public' and floated a new holding company on the stock

J. R. Hugh Sumner, son of the founder of Typhoo.

No. 1
The Gorilla
The largest of the apes; possesses immense strength and surprising agility. Chiefly vegetarian in diet but can be extremely ferocious. Most of its life is spent in the tree tops. Inhabits limited areas of Central and West Africa.

Ty-phoo Tea Series of 20

No. 1
Houses of Parliament
With its imposing towers and many pinnacles, the Royal Palace of Westminster containing the two Houses of Parliament is one of the world's most famous buildings. Covering eight acres, the Palace was designed by Sir Charles Barry after the fire of 1834.

Ty-phoo Tea Series of 20

No. 1
Airedale Terrier
As its name implies, the Airedale originated in Yorkshire, where some sportsmen crossed a working terrier strain with Otterhound. The Airedale is the largest British terrier and is a great favourite with both grown-ups and children.

Ty-Phoo Tea Series of 20

No. 1
Aircraft Carrier
These great ships are like floating aerodromes, complete with repair shops, fuel tanks and hangar space. H.M.S. *Eagle* and H.M.S. *Ark Royal* have a displacement of 36,800 tons and can carry from 80 to 110 aircraft.

Ty-phoo Tea Series of 20

No. 1
Niagara Falls
Unrivalled for grandeur and beauty, the great falls of the Niagara river between U.S.A. and Canada are actually two distinct cataracts. Illustrated is Horseshoe Fall, whose curve of water (over 2,000 ft.) plunges 158 ft. into the gorge below.

Ty-phoo Tea Series of 20

A selection of post-war tea packet cards.

Leonard Goode supervises the discharge of chests from barge into warehouse at Typhoo's own private canal wharf.

exchange. 'Typhoo Tea (Holdings) Limited', as it was called, acquired the whole of the issue share capital of 'Typhoo Tea Limited' which had been a private limited company since 1905, and The Meriden Tea Company Limited with its subsidiary Tea Buyers Limited. The flotation was a success; all the shares, Cumulative Preference and Ordinary, were taken up; the first year's profits exceeded expectations.

The company, along with its competitors, was now on the brink of wooing the tea-drinking public to buy *its* brand in preference to others with an unrestricted promotional campaign of the kind that had made 'Typhoo' a household name between the wars. They could no longer push the digestive qualities of Typhoo, but on to the sides of their packets they began once more to print the series of picture postcards which had been so popular before the war and proved as great an attraction to children after it. Throughout the nineteen fifties there were series of Wild Animals, Famous Buildings, Common British Birds, Popular Breeds of Dogs, Types of Ships, Famous Bridges and World Wonders. This helped give the boost which, with the abolition of wartime Food Rationing in 1952, the company was looking for. With Ceylon still unable to supply all the company hoped to order, buying and shipping arrangements were made with India – with Matheson & Co. in Calcutta and Matheson & Bosanquet & Co. in Cochin. A shipping department was formed to cope with the documentation, payment of freight, clearance and delivery to warehouse, and the shipping and marine insurance claims. Delivery of tea from depots inside Britain ceased to be by canal barge, and was taken over by British Road Service vehicles.

They installed new packing machines inside the factory to cope with the increased output. Sales took off and 1954's profit of £675,000 became £842,016 in 1955. Tea chests which carried 50 lb of packed tea gave way to 25 lb and 50 lb 'fiberites' which were packed automatically, sealed and sent off by overhead conveyor to the warehouse for despatch. Automatic packing machines dealt with quarter pound packets of Typhoo tea by the million, each containing only one blend.

Typhoo along with others had to resort to mixing blends when, in 1955, housewives read in their papers of the condemnation by Sir John Kotalawa, prime minister of Ceylon, of the cost of tea in London. 'It was damn ridiculous,' he said, 'that tea which cost three shillings a pound in Colombo was priced at seven shillings in London.' The British price was not as damn ridiculous as Sir John insisted. He forgot to mention the 1s 11½d per pound export duty imposed by his government, and all the unavoidable freight, insurance and handling charges. However in the hope of Sir John's remarks causing the price of tea to drop, the ladies stopped buying tea, and kept their teapots filled with the contents of packets already stored in the kitchen cupboard. The price of tea in Britain *did* drop, and companies like Typhoo were left with large stocks which they had purchased at the higher market price and had to blend at loss until they could even out prices with tea bought at the lowest market values.

But this was a mere hiccup, and by 1960 Typhoo had become brand leader in the grocery trade, and the £2,730,000 profit of that year was a record. It was a success story that was bound to attract a takeover bid – and sure enough one came from the American group General Foods which owned Birds Custard and Maxwell House coffee. They offered to buy Typhoo Holdings, paying 40 per cent in cash and the balance in dollar shares which had an equivalent English value of about £21 a share. The chairman told the annual general meeting of February 1961 that the high price of each American share would have made it very difficult to allocate them to the many small shareholders in the company, and 'as it appeared that the Treasury were not in favour of the deal, negotiations were terminated.'

There was little the management could do however to ward off the troubles which arose from the Chinese invasion of the North East frontier of India, and a strike of workers on the Brahmaputra River, which upset the flow of tea to Calcutta and brought the price of tea on the world market soaring. But once again, however worrying they seemed at the time, these occurrences proved mere hiccups and, with the Indo-Chinese ceasefire and the settlement of the strike, the status quo was thankfully restored – and Typhoo's trading profit rose to £3,223,000. Shareholders received one free share for every five they held.

Typhoo were now packing more than eighty million pounds of tea every year, and a significant proportion of that was being exported to some 40 countries throughout the world. To pack the increased bulk of tea for home and overseas consumption they invested over £83,000 in the latest sophisticated packing machinery which filled a packet every second.

Originally Typhoo tea had been shipped in 70 lb wooden, lead-lined chests. After World War II these had given way to plywood chests lined with aluminium foil and paper holding some 110 lb of bulk tea. But the quality of plywood deteriorated, and tea chests became so brittle they had to be handled with the greatest care if they were not to be damaged, and that lost the company time and money. When flimsy tea chests of this sort were shipped 'break bulk', the vessels were filled to capacity with loose chests so that it became a huge floating tea warehouse. If

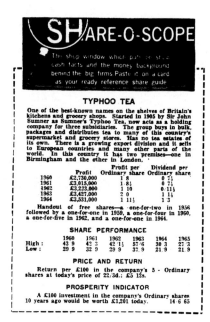

Typhoo's consistent good performance was featured by a national newspaper.

the cargo was not stowed securely, then any movement during the voyage could result in damage and loss of tea, particularly if heavy weather was encountered. Sometimes during unloading dockers might use hooks to lift out difficult chests. A neat hole caused by the hook would be left in the chest and, if not repaired, could result in tea trailing along the motorways like gunpowder from a barrel.

Pallets were used at the Bordesley Street works throughout the nineteen twenties to move stock about the premises, but not until the nineteen sixties were they introduced for transporting tea chests from the country of origin to Britain. Twenty tea chests were strapped to the pallet by metal or plastic bands so they travelled the whole way to the UK as a single unit. It resulted in far less damage, and East African countries quickly cottoned on to the idea, though palletisation was more slowly adopted by India and Ceylon. Later it became a matter of stacking some 200 palletised tea chests – or maybe 230 loose chests of tea into a 20 ft container.

The nineteen sixties was a period of immense activity and a heavy investment programme was undertaken from the unload-

A busy line produces a continuous supply of quarter-pound packets of Typhoo.

ing bay through blending, packing and despatch departments. General Manager Fred Parkin recalls how one of the most efficient lines they had was six automatic packing machines, each delivering two streams of tea on to a long conveyor. 'We had 12 streams of tea moving down the factory to one end, where an automatic machine parcelled them into 5 lb parcels. At peak periods there were 64 quarter pound packing machines in operation. It was a wonderful development.'

Innovation in administration matched technological developments. The cash-with-order (CWO) system introduced in 1920 by Sir John Sumner had stood the test of time, its benefits shared by both the company and Typhoo's customers. But in the nineteen sixties fierce competition compelled Typhoo to start offering credit facilities. It was a sign of the times that Chairman J. R. Hugh Sumner told shareholders at the 1965 annual general meeting that the outstanding debt to the company had risen to

H. C. Kelley became chairman of Typhoo Tea (Holdings) in 1966, following J. R. Hugh Sumner who retired at the age of 80.

Mr A. J. Pendry, Typhoo's first tea buyer and blender in 1934 tests a batch in the original tea tasting department.

LET'S FACE IT! by Lewis Williams

" Yoo-hoo . . . . . Typhoo : "

Lewis Williams, cartoonist for The Birmingham Evening Mail *cleverly combines Typhoo with Schweppes.*

more than £2 million. Even so, in keeping with the late Sir John Sumner's practice of each year investing some of the company's profits in securities, by 1963 the management had £3,575,000 invested in cash loans to local authorities which brought in a very satisfactory return. And the pre-tax profit continued to rise – from £3,400,000 in 1964 to £3,640,000 in 1965.

It was in this time of Typhoo's rising fortunes that the chairman, J. R. Hugh Sumner, reached the age of 80, and decided to hand over the chairmanship, which he had held since the death of his father in 1934, to managing director H. C. Kelley who was able to announce at his first AGM in April 1967 that Typhoo had earned a pre-tax profit of £3,939,646.

Such consistently good results, together with reserves of around £5 million, meant that more and more companies were eyeing the rich independent Typhoo company as a valuable potential asset. For six months at the end of 1967 the directors of Typhoo entered into talks with Lord Watkinson, managing director of Schweppes, the famous old established soft drinks firm, which Jacob Schweppe had set up at Ye Old Fountain House, Bristol in 1790 to manufacture high quality carbonated water. No news of the negotiations leaked out to the media or City financial circles and, while they were going on, Typhoo declared a £4,140,000 profit for 1967, and Schweppes £5,900,000.

The *Financial Times* called it 'one of the best kept merger secrets for some time' when it was announced on 24 January 1968 that Typhoo was to join Schweppes' old Food Division to form a new company called 'Typhoo Schweppes'. The brands

The Birmingham Post *reports on the merger of Typhoo and Schweppes.*

£45m takeover bid for Typhoo Tea

An agreed £45m takeover bid has been made for Typhoo Tea (Holdings), the Birmingham-based group, which is one of Britain's biggest tea firms, by Schweppes, the soft drinks combine.

The terms, which are recommended to shareholders by the chairman, Mr. H. C. Kelley, and his co-directors, put a value of 35s. 6d. on Typhoo shares, which stood in the stock market last night at 30s.

If the deal goes through, the two concerns will form a grouping worth £110m. Former Typhoo holders will own 41 per cent of the shares, and those of Schweppes, 59 per cent.

It is planned that Typhoo—

Birmingham Post City Staff

the firm which "puts the T in Britain"—and the food interests Schweppes (including Chivers James) will join forces in a new Typhoo-Schweppes subsidiary.

Mr. H. C. Kelley and Mr. J. P. Tustain will join the main Schweppes board and the board of Typhoo-Schweppes, of which Mr. P. D. Kelley will also be a director.

Between them, the Typhoo directors and their families hold 12p.c. of the Typhoo shares.

Merger talks—in which neither side will admit to taking the initiative—were started three months ago and speeded up in the last two weeks.

The secret was well kept and

no flicker of a leak disturbed the Typhoo share price.

One question which must arise is the possibility of a counter bid.

In 1960, Kraft Foods of America made a takeover approach on the basis of an offer not much above the present Typhoo price.

After careful thought by the Typhoo board with its City advisers, negotiations were discontinued.

There is some indication that American concerns may more recently have felt interest in Typhoo, though a counter-offer from such a source must be considered less likely since President Johnson's curbs on United States overseas investment.

Company Affairs—
Page 5.

of the new division included Schweppes, Hartley, Chivers and Moorhouse, together with the Kia-Ora soft drink range and Harveys of Belgravia canned foods. It was said that the merger would give Typhoo an entry into the American market in which Schweppes was heavily involved; but more attractive for Schweppes was the opportunity to broaden their home base at a time when they were in danger of becoming too top heavy with overseas interests.

Chairman of Typhoo Schweppes, whose role was to co-ordinate

The memorial stone at the family vault in Coleshill churchyard.

J. P. Tustain.

the activities of Schweppes (Foods) Limited and Typhoo Tea Limited, was James Barker, whose appointment along with the rest of the Board was announced in May. One of the directors was H. C. Kelley who had been chairman of Typhoo Tea (Holdings) Limited who resigned from that position in September, while remaining a director of Schweppes. James Barker took his place as chairman of the holdings company, with J. P. Tustain and W. F. Lewis as joint managing directors. John Black Sumner, grandson of the founder and the last of the Sumner family to be actively involved with the company, took the opportunity provided by the merger with Schweppes to withdraw and devote himself to his many other outside interests and to Trust work. His father J. R. Hugh Sumner who was 81 in 1968 – the son of the founder – was living in retirement at Droitwich running a farm and breeding racehorses – and there four years later he died. [3]

Thus, 65 years after Sir John Sumner had launched the Typhoo brand of tea which was to become so popular, the one-product, one-brand operation had become part of an altogether bigger exercise – and with the purchase by Schweppes of the Kenco Coffee Company from Trust Houses in 1969 for £2 million, it found itself in an even bigger group.

Within a short time, however, Lord Watkinson and his colleagues were setting their sights even higher. At the end of January 1969 they concluded a merger with Adrian Cadbury

J. B. Sumner, grandson of the founder.

and Cadburys, which had been started by John Cadbury as tea dealers in Bull Street, Birmingham in 1824, and then gone on to sell the cocoa and chocolate for which the company, now based at Bournville, had become world renowned. The two companies were convinced that such a merger would be to their mutual benefit in the creation of a strong international organisation ranking high among world companies. The new group known as Cadbury Schweppes had Lord Watkinson as chairman and Adrian Cadbury as deputy chairman. It had capital employed of £150 million, an annual turnover of £250 million and trading profits of more than £20 million – six million of which came from overseas sales. Schweppes offered 15 of its own five shilling shares for every four of Cadbury's £1 ordinary shares. The bid was worth around £116 million and ranked Cadbury Schweppes eighth in the world league table of food companies. The Board of Trade had no objection, and there was no question of referring the merger to the Monopolies Commission.

Typhoo now had another brand of tea being sold by its own marketing organisation – the 'Fine Brew' an instant tea which Cadburys were packing at their Moreton Wirral factory. Otherwise there was very little overlap of products as a result of the Cadbury Schweppes merger. The merger slowly began to take shape. The group was restructured into six divisions: Overseas, Confectionery, Retail, Company Services, Food, and Tea & Coffee which consisted of Typhoo Tea and Kenco Coffee and was headed by J. P. Tustain. In 1970, some 45 million cups were being made with Typhoo blended and packed at Bordesley Street. A third well-known brand of tea and coffee was acquired by Cadbury Schweppes with the purchase from Fortes Holdings of Kardomah, a company founded by the Vey brothers in Liverpool.

Distribution of the factory's output was severely hampered

An in-store display.

With trams disappearing from the streets of Britain in the 1950s, Typhoo were still able to use buses to carry their message. Here, a London Transport bus displays the famous 'Yoo-Hoo, Typhoo' advertisement, which also incorporates the slogan 'Typhoo puts the "T" in Britain'.

112

in 1972 when a national dock strike started and closed almost all of Britain ports. Ships had to abandon their cargoes at what their masters considered the nearest port, which was rarely convenient for the cargo owner. Thousands of chests of tea were dumped in Denmark, France, Germany, Belgium, Holland and Portugal, and had to be stored wherever there was space which more often than not turned out to be highly unsuitable and frequently somewhat bizarre.

When the strike was called off, owners had to organise the return of their own cargo, and pay the additional freight to have it shipped back to Britain. The Tea Trade appointed a co-ordinating committee to identify and monitor the return of the abandoned cargoes for those who felt unable to do it for themselves. Inevitably many consignments suffered from poor

MV. Wladyslaw Lokietek – one of the few vessels to unload at Liverpool. This cargo consisted of sixty-five containers of tea for Typhoo from Mombasa.

storage conditions and rough handling of tea chests; and too many returned to base badly damaged. There was very much less damage to abandoned cargoes during the next national dock strike in 1975 for by then most tea was being shipped in containers in which they remained quite safely on the continental quays on which they had been dumped, protected from the elements and irresponsible handlers. Much goodwill was created between shipping companies and cargo owners by the former returning many of the containers at their own expense.

By 1984 most consignments of tea coming into Britain were in 20-foot containers holding 200 chests on ten pallets. A 40-foot container held double the quantity, but unless it could be taken from ship's side to warehouse by rail, as was done from Felixstowe and Southampton to Dagenham Storage, the cab, unit and load of the motor vehicle would be likely to exceed the legal axle weight limit for British roads which was 38.5 tonnes. Its load would have to be lightened before being allowed on the road.

The introduction of containers had considerable effect on the old established tea ports of Britain. The preparations taken at Felixstowe to handle them, and the good labour relations prevailing at this 'free' port, helped to attract shipping lines away from Liverpool, Avonmouth and other ports. In the nineteen eighties most ships from East Africa and India discharge their tea there. Tea from South Africa and the Far East is mostly discharged at the port of Southampton which has deep water terminals and excellent road-rail links. A considerable amount of container cargo moves through the port of London at Tilbury. The big container operators OCL and ACT discharge tea at

Typhoo's gnu.

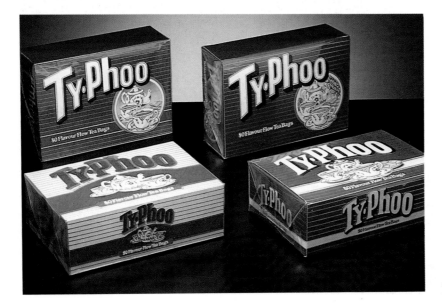

The early Typhoo tea bags.

Felixstowe, Southampton and London.

To meet the new circumstances created by containerisation Customs & Excise built inland container terminals, like that at Northampton serving Felixstowe, to speed up proceedings. The initial fears of the dockers that they would lose their jobs soon died away. Typhoo's decision to take as much cargo as possible, within prescribed limits, direct from vessels into the Moreton factory brought changes in warehousing procedures. A certain amount of outside storage was still required, but the company were able to make considerable savings. Capital was also released by reducing tea stocks.

Computerisation of hitherto manually kept account books, staff records, sales data and the rest brought further changes. It meant a great saving in the number of clerical staff employed. Whereas in the days of bulk shipping eight clerks had been needed, using computers the department was reduced to three – a manager, his assistant and a clerk.

Administrative re-structuring within Cadbury Schweppes took a further step in January 1973 when they formed a Tea & Food Group which embraced Marvel, Smash, Chivers, Moorhouse, Hartley preserves, jellies, canned fruit and vegetables, Cadbury biscuits and beverages and, what was their

Mr E. H. Pedvin and Joe Taylor are here tasting a batch with the tea girls in attendance in the tea tasting department alongside the canal at Bordesley Street.

single biggest brand, Typhoo Tea. The new Tea & Food Group within Cadbury Schweppes, of which J. T. Beasley was chairman, had a turnover of £70 million and a combined labour force of 7,000.

The tea drinkers of Britain had begun to show their preference to making their habitual nice cup of tea with tea bags rather than loose tea, and the marketing men found that sales of Typhoo in packets was losing ground to their competitors who had been early into tea-bag production. From February 1972 a new and bigger tea bag was launched supported by a £200,000 advertising campaign on television and in the trade press. To make up for lost time a study team was appointed to consider ways and means of converting the Bordesley Street plant into the most modern tea bag and packet tea factory in Europe.

What ensued was a strategic review of the production facilities required to meet the fiercely competitive tea market. Initial proposals to extend and reorganise Bordesley Street starting in April 1974 foundered following the refusal of the Transport and General Workers Union and Cadbury Schweppes to compromise on a fundamental change in shift patterns. By July 1974 a tea plant was to be installed at Moreton on Merseyside. Apart from the emergency blend packed for the Company when the factory was bombed in 1941, this would be the first time in the Company's history that Typhoo blend had been packed outside Birmingham.

Finally in November 1978 production at Bordesley Street came to a halt and for once the tea dust would be allowed to settle as production was transferred entirely to the Moreton site.

The closure of the Typhoo tea factory at Bordesley Street did not mean an end to the reorganisation of the Cadbury Schweppes Tea & Food Division. Sweeping changes were introduced in May 1979 with the aim of dramatically reducing running costs. Cadbury Schweppes had made a healthy £48 million profit in 1978, and the Tea & Food Division had made a considerable contribution to it. But it had not itself attained the level of profit which had been set as its target.

So the activities of Cadbury Typhoo Limited, Cadbury Schweppes Foods Limited, Typhoo Tea Limited and Franklin Foods Limited were merged, and their trading operations were transferred to Cadbury Schweppes Foods Limited. The Meriden Tea Company became a subsidiary of Cadbury Schweppes; and Kenco Coffee Company became a direct subsidiary of that company. Cadbury Typhoo Tea and Franklin Foods became its dormant subsidiaries. Meriden Tea continued to buy its own tea, but from 1979 the whole of Cadbury Schweppes Tea & Food Division was made part of Cadbury Typhoo Limited.

In 1979 Typhoo Tea was launched in a way that would give it maximum consumer impact – a new blend in a new pack trumpeted abroad by a massive – and massively expensive – television advertising campaign, supported by one of the grocery trade's largest sampling operations – in the single month of August 1981 six million free samples of Ty-phoo Tea (enough to make two pots) were delivered to houses all over Britain. To each packet was attached a coupon which the recipient could present to her grocer and receive another packet of Typhoo at a discount of fivepence.

The relaunch was the climax of two years' market research and product development which had revealed that there was still a big demand for 'quality packet tea' (as opposed to tea bags), the market for which was valued at £135 million. Very

Page 8, Tea & Foods News, September 1981

Six million samples — and a guarantea, re-launch Typhoo

A NEW pack, a new blend, a massive television advertising campaign, and one of the grocery trade's largest sampling drops marked the relaunch of Typhoo Tea.

During August, six million samples packed at Moreton each incorporating a money-off coupon and enough tea to make two pots, were delivered to households. In the same month, four million leaflets giving a 'guarantea' — the offer of a free sample, together with a 5p off coupon — were distributed.

Together, these 10 million coupons and samples will ensure immediate awareness of the new pack and a high level of consumer trial of the newly blended tea.

In addition, a nationwide television advertising campaign will be seen by most households in the country many times before the end of the year.

This relaunch follows an extensive two year market research and product development campaign. Surveys showed there is a continuing high demand of quality packet tea, which many people believe to be the only product offering a value for money, traditional high quality brew.

Among the characteristics of the new blend are a quicker performance and a more golden colour. However, only marginal changes have been made to the blend's flavour which also had a high acceptance rating in the extensive tests preceding the relaunch.

Although the overall market for packet tea is gradually declining marketing and sales director Mike Newitt, is optimistic about the future: "The packet tea market is vital for grocers, and at £135 million is still substantially larger than, for example, the entire baked bean or fruit squash markets.

"Our two year consumer research programme revealed that the quality of packet tea is an important factor. Typhoo was consistently rated to be of superior quality to other packet teas, confirming the brand's strong association with the tea drinking heritage and traditions in Britain," explained Mr Newitt.

"As one of the first companies to sell packet tea, we have over 75 years' experience of consumer requirements and are in an ideal position to lead the market's development over the next decade to ensure Typhoo retains its position as today's traditional taste."

June Johnson, pictured on the Moreton Typhoo packing line approves of the new pack. "I think it is more appealing than the one it replaces," she told News. June has worked at the Wirral factory for nine years.

little change was made to the flavour of the 1981 Typhoo, but it had a more golden colour and brewed more quickly.

Blend sheets were still prepared by the Tea Department at Bournville and sent to Moreton for action; but the new machinery and extra operators ensured that the flow of both packeted loose tea and the shrink-wrapped boxes of tea bags operated without interruption. The early 1980s was a period when the price of tea in auctions around the world was rising at a dramatic rate. In the last months of 1983 tea was being sold at twice the price it had been 12 months earlier. Marketing expertise was required as never before – and sophisticated marketing administrative skills to handle the increasingly competitive market place. The rise in raw tea costs continued into 1984 with Indian Government intervention reducing the available supplies of tea. Each and every tea producer had to learn to become more cost effective and soften the blow faced by consumers in rising shelf prices.

A silver tea pot presented to Typhoo by Ceylon agents Carson Cumberbatch & Co. Ltd in honour of fifty years' mutually successful trading.

TY·PHOO

7. New Horizons

IN 1986 possibly one of the most exciting stages occurred in the history of Typhoo. Cadbury Schweppes had made known its intention to concentrate on their main core business, worldwide confectionery and soft drinks. By January 1986 negotiations were well advanced between Cadbury Schweppes and the existing Cadbury Typhoo board, plus P. R. Judge, Planning Director of Cadbury Schweppes concerning a Management buyout.

In the face of fierce competition from third parties, the buyout team supported by the entire workforce successfully gained control of Beverages and Foods Division and registered a private limited company on 24 March 1986 under the name 'Premier Brands Limited'. They signed all the agreements covering the transfer of the business to them from Cadbury Schweppes on 25 April. Final financial details were settled by 18 May. Premier Brands were the successors in management to a business with a turnover of £311.1 million which in the 12 months leading to the take-over had earned a profit of £6.8 million. Every effort was now directed at maintaining that level of earning – and if possible lifting it even higher. The business which Premier Brands now managed was what had been Cadbury Schweppes's Tea & Food Divison in the UK, and its Food Division in Ireland and France. 'Independence Day' was 13 May 1986. The company achieved and enjoyed an immense feeling of identity and motivation which itself was fuelled by the outstanding progress made in its financial results. The strategy was clearly set as growth from both existing product opportunities and acquisitions.

In the early stages major exercises were completed in 'domestic housekeeping' in order to establish independence and address the balance sheet and profit issues. The Kenco Coffee Company was sold to General Foods Limited who took over the entire staff of 150 in the Earlsfield Factory and 35 sales staff. What clearly followed for the tea business was a purposeful push to achieve the group goal of growth.

The acquisition trail actively pursued by the tea business opened with Melroses being added in November 1986. The famous Scottish tea company was founded in Edinburgh in 1812 and possesses the largest speciality tea processing facility in Scotland. The tea factory they had built in 1927 was on the historic site of the ancient citadel of Leith. They had been granted the Royal Warrant in 1837 and it had been confirmed by each succeeding monarch. No strangers to Typhoo, Melroses had been packing Typhoo's 'Catering 250' packs for some time, and plans were afoot for a Melrose Tea export range. The Scottish firm had already increased its output by November 1987, added extra shifts, taken on more people and made a bigger trading profit in its first half year under Premier Brands direction than it had made in the previous full 12 months.

But this was only the first of four acquisitions by the new management in 1986–7. The second was of the Glengettie Tea Company, operating predominantly in the private label field and comprising three manufacturing companies, David Lloyd Piggot, Chiltern and Charter, as well as the Brown White tea

The ornate tea service presented to Thomas Ridgway by the Birmingham creditors.

broking operation. Glengettie also had a 52 per cent share in another tea broker, J. Upcot (Africa) Limited. It had three factories – in Glasgow, Leighton Buzzard and London – and around 300 employees. The Glengettie brand of tea was strong in Wales and in the west of England.

This second acquisition increased the volume of Premier Brands in the UK tea market so as to place it after Brooke Bond but ahead of Lyons and Tetley.

The third brand of tea to join the group was Ridgways – premium and speciality teas blended and packed at Speke near Liverpool by a workforce of some 150 – which Premier Brands bought from Tate & Lyle. Thomas Ridgway became a partner of Arthur Dakin Co., grocers, of 14 Bull Ring, Birmingham, in the eighteen twenties. Thomas Ridgway and Arthur Dakin will have known William Sumner, grandfather of the founder of Typhoo whose grocers shop lay across the road at 97 High Street, Bull Ring. When Dakin's company went bankrupt in 1836, Ridgway moved to London where he set up his own grocery business which became very much more successful than Dakin's in Birmingham. Within a short time he was able to repay all the money still owed to creditors in Birmingham, and to show their gratitude they presented him with an ornate tea service which Premier Brands have to this day. Of even greater value they have Ridgways' royal Warrant as supplier of tea to Her Majesty Queen Elizabeth II and Her Majesty the Queen Mother. The first of Ridgways' Royal warrants was granted in 1886 when Queen Victoria asked for a special blend for her own use. The company called this Her Majesty's Blend – and it is still being produced a hundred years later.

Two non-tea companies were acquired in September 1987 at the same time as Ridgways – Newtime Foods and British Food Canners – and these greatly strengthened Premier Brands' presence in the food market. The fourth tea company to be acquired was the Jersey Trading Corporation SrL, the largest tea manufacturer in Italy.

The new management were justifiably proud of what they had achieved in so short a time. Reviewing Premier Brands' performance during its first year the company reported a trading

Shown here are the three royal warrants proudly possessed by Melroses and Ridgways. Both companies are now part of Premier Brands.

BY APPOINTMENT
TO HER MAJESTY THE QUEEN
PURVEYORS OF TEA & COFFEE
MELROSES LTD EDINBURGH

BY APPOINTMENT TO
HER MAJESTY QUEEN ELIZABETH
THE QUEEN MOTHER
TEA & COFFEE MERCHANTS
RIDGWAYS LONDON

BY APPOINTMENT TO
HER MAJESTY QUEEN ELIZABETH II
TEA MERCHANTS
RIDGWAYS LONDON

The original branded range.

The acquisition trail continued with the Glengette Tea Company in early 1987.

By November 1986 the product range had expanded to include the famous Scottish tea company, Melroses, founded in 1812.

By late 1987 the range was further expanded by the addition of Ridgways.

123

Ty·Phoo

THE GREAT TEDDY BEARS' PICNIC

In Aid Of The National Children's Home
BANK HOLIDAY MONDAY 31st AUGUST 1987
KNEBWORTH PARK 10.30 am–5.30 pm

Free with the compliments of Typhoo.
Includes entrance to Knebworth House, gardens, park,
fort and adventure playground.

Parachuting Teddies · Teddy Bear Balloon Race · Teddy Bear Treasure Hunt · Gipsy Ted Lee · Paw Readings · Teddy Bear Hospital · Teddy Bear Artists · Teddy Bear

Bring Your Teddy Bear and a picnic!

Auction · Famous Character Bears · Celebrity Teddies · Enter the Typhoo Bear of the Year Awards · Free Competitions · Giveaways · Prizes · And lots, lots more!

A card advertises Typhoo's Great Teddy Bears' Picnic at Knebworth Park. The event raised thousands of pounds for the National Children's Home.

The tradition set by Sir John Sumner, founder of Typhoo, in supporting charitable causes is carried on enthusiastically by the present administration.
Some of the 33,000 participants in the 25 mile Birmingham Walkathon are seen entering one of the many free tea stations placed around the route by Typhoo. The company helped sponsor the event in 1987 which raised more than £400,000 for charity.

Always a popular attraction wherever they appear throughout the country, Typhoo's mad hatter and giant walking tea pot are here photographed during the 1986 Birmingham Show at Perry Park.

In 1987 the Duke of Edinburgh visited Melroses on the occasion of their 175th anniversary.

profit of £16½ million, reversing the decline of the previous three years. Each part of the company had contributed to the successful trading of 1986, but their results still depended to a regrettable extent on the price of tea. Borrowings had been reduced by £19 million, but they still owed a very considerable sum from the original buyout cost £97 million, the servicing of which cost £8 million in interest – more than £1,000 an hour. That was the price of independence.

Some of the exciting products provided by the leading UK Herbal Tea Company, London Herb and Spice.

Significant profit improvement were a key feature of the consecutive years. A time in which the tea operation expanded its interests further by acquiring the herbal tea market leader, London Herb & Spice. A company which had 70 per cent of the fast growing herbal tea market whose brand name included LHS, Heath and Heather and Secret Garden.

Internal growth from existing products and the innovative One Cup concept and Typhoo Q Tea instant white tea added to the Group's performance.

In January 1989 the company was the proud recipient of an award presented by Baroness Trumpington, Parliamentary Secretary (Lords) for Ministry of Agriculture, Fisheries and Food of the '1989 Grocer/IFE Business Award' to recognise business excellence, beating many of the well established giants in the food and drinks industry. An award won on building on the views of the Sumner founders for financial performance, development of trading relations with customers, excellence in staff development, innovation in product development and range

Typhoo's one cup and Q.T. innovations in the tea trade set the standard for others to follow. Shown here in their original livery.

extension, success in merger and acquisition activity, and overall business enterprise.

The introduction of a new foil pack in mid-1989 saw the first significant change in the tea market in many years.

Featured here is the Typhoo pack in its new livery. The launch also covered Melroses, Ridgways, Glengette and Fresh Brew brands.

Under the new ownership of Hillsdown Holdings PLC Premier Brands, of which Typhoo is an integral part, encouragement for independence linked with continued growth is paramount, and on what is now a complex business innovation allied to an understanding of customer needs remains as true today with the present Board/Management as in John Sumner's day.

While John Sumner's Bank had overlooked the most important asset, the man behind the balance sheet, Hillsdown have looked at both the company and those in charge and like what they see. With such dedicated pioneers the future of Premier Brands and of 'Typhoo' Tea, Birmingham's premier tea company seems assured.

The present management team: (from left to right) W. J. King, Speciality Tea Director; P. R. Rigg, Financial Controller; A. C. M. Harrisson, Buying Director; M. J. E. Gill, Export Director; D. D. Reid, Tea Managing Director; D. C. Greig, Herbal Tea Director; P. W. G. Davis, Mainstream Tea Director; J. R. Gothard, Sales Director; C. J. Tugman, NPD Director.

INDEX

INDEX

INDEX

The PLAN of BIRMIN

Cold Bath

The Parfonage

Smallbrook Street

Finkles Street

Dudly Street

Worcester Street

Edgbaston Street

Lea Lane

Mercer or Spicer Street

St. John's

High Town

Corn Market

Corn Cheaping

Moor Street

Cook or Well Street

Park Street

Digbeth

Lower Mill Lane

Moat or Mill Lane

Scale of Ten Perch or 55 Yards

Bracoll Head

The River Rea

Digbeth

Deretend

The River Rea

In the Year 1700 Birmingham Contained 30 Streets, 100 Courts and Alleys, 2504 Houses, 15032 Inhabitants, one Church dedicated to St. Martin & a Chappel to St. John, & a School founded by Edward 6th also 2 Dissenting Meeting Houses.

the
Edwd Digby
Members
for the Co
this Plate is hi
by their moft obe
The Plate is the Poffeffion of Thing